The Forests of Great Smoky Mountains National Park

A Naturalist's Guide to Understanding and Identifying Southern Appalachian Forest Types

Dan D. Williams MS

Cover Painting and Design by James Richards

http://jrichardsstudio.com/

To George
A fellow plant enthusiast
Best Regards
Dan

Possum Publications, Athens Georgia

All topographic maps used in this book are from
Google Maps.com

Great Smoky Mountains National Park official map is
used as the base map for the two overlay maps in this
book with permission from the Great Smoky
Mountains Association.

ISBN : 1451564988

EAN-13: 9781451564983

THE WEB SITE

Full color versions of all maps and graphs contained in the book, and a photographic tree identification guide are available for free download from:

http://www.forestsofgreatsmokymountains.com/

ACKNOWLEDGEMENTS

Many people contributed to the knowledge contained in this book. My parents encouraged me to learn. Siblings became willing partners in the search for knowledge. Teachers on all levels supplied the information and motivation needed to reach higher. Associates at the Warnell School of Forestry and Natural Resources willingly engaged in the exchange of information. Thank you all!

Special thanks goes to Jenny Williams, Lauren Williams, Dr. Walter L. Cook and Dr. Scott Merkle, each of whom edited most of the book.

Thanks also to Dr. Bob Tesky, Dr. Lindsay Boring and Tom Remelay for assisting with specific book sections.

Additional thanks to David, Ginger, Manuel and to Bill Lott who freely shares his dendrological knowledge. Also to Jim Richards for the wonderful cover painting and design, Carolyn Marquez for the excellent web page, and finally to Lisa and Harry, world's greatest hiking partners.

Table of Contents

INTRODUCTION

What is biodiversity? Simply put it is the variety of life found in a particular place, and there is a particular place in the backyard of Eastern America renowned for its biodiversity. It is called Great Smoky Mountains National Park (GSMNP). The Park's half million acres nurture and protect over 15,000 different life forms, both plant and animal, and the search for new life there continues. Referred to by many as wildflower national park, this sanctuary of verdant valleys and rugged peaks supports more kinds of flowering plants than any other national park. It could as easily be called salamander national park with 30 species of these diminutive creatures thriving in its moist hollows, or ancient forest national park with its 100,000 acres of centuries-old undisturbed forest: a claim unrivaled east of the Mississippi River.

This rich but rugged landscape was originally the realm of the Cherokee Indian who hunted its game with stone-tipped arrows and gave its ridges mysterious names like "Frog Place." The settlers that followed soon learned the rich black ground of valley bottoms yielded corn taller than a man, and that every autumn walnuts, hickory nuts and chestnuts fell in immense numbers from trees a whole family of barefoot kids couldn't reach around. Young girls knew an Easter Sunday stroll through woods and fields revealed wildflowers in profusion matching the colors of the rainbow. Even the corporate loggers who came later recognized the vast and varied forest riches that could be extracted from this natural sanctuary, where the number and size of valuable lumber trees was staggering.

These mountain forests are among the most varied and diverse to be found anywhere. Nearly every major forest type in the eastern U. S. grows within the Park's borders, and that brings us to the topic of this book. A good description of what the book is begins by telling what it isn't. It isn't a research paper written for publication in a science journal. Neither is it a general guide book to the Smokies. It is something in between. This book attempts to digest much of the immense amount of excellent research conducted on the Park's forests and condense it into a form more easily understood by individuals interested in becoming actively involved in learning more about the forest treasures found here.

Four important factors have shaped the forests of GSMNP and the southern Appalachians. These factors are <u>elevation, landform, forest age</u> and <u>exotic tree diseases</u>. This book discusses the influence of each factor on the Park's present-day forests and teaches the reader how to interpret them.

The first chapters define elevation and landform and discuss their role as nature's tools in shaping mountain forests. Chapter four presents the Forest Finder, a graphical representation of the major forest types of Great Smoky Mountains National Park. The Forest Finder graphically illustrates the influence of elevation and landform on forest types, and provides an easy-to-use guide for locating and understanding the forest types encountered on Park visits. The Forest Finder is applicable to all southern Appalachian forests.

Later chapters explain how man's activities have profoundly affected the forests of GSMNP and other areas of the southern Appalachians. Chapter five shows how farming and logging during the past 200 years cleared the land, turning the forest succession clock back to time zero. The process of forest succession is explained, and the reader learns how to use this knowledge to read the forest and determine its successional stage and approximate age. Chapter eight tells the story of tree diseases from other parts of the world, and how they have devastated GSMNP forests, drastically altering forest makeup.

Other practical skills for learning about the Park's forests are also included in the book, such as, accessing and printing topographic maps from the internet, measuring trees, pacing distances, sampling the forest, and more. The goal is to equip you, the reader, with practical knowledge and skill to help you develop a deeper level of understanding, enjoyment and appreciation for the forests of GSMNP, the world's stellar example of southern Appalachian forests.

This book assists the reader in learning to identify many of the trees found in the Park, a rewarding but possibly daunting prospect for the beginner. The book contains a list of the Park's major trees, as well as sections describing most of them. We challenge the reader to dive in head-first and embrace wholeheartedly the study of GSMNP trees and the forests where they grow. The intellectual, recreational and emotional paybacks are immense and life changing.

CHAPTER 1. ELEVATION

Elevation is the vertical height above sea level of a particular place. Elevation has the greatest influence on the forests of Great Smoky Mountains National Park (GSMNP). As the mountain traveler ascends, air gets cooler. In fact, every one thousand-foot increase in elevation causes a temperature decrease of about 3.5 degrees Fahrenheit. Two reasons account for this correlation between temperature and elevation. First, air is warmed not by the sun, but by the earth's surface. The sun warms the earth; then, the earth warms the air. Flat land absorbs and re-radiates much more of the sun's warmth than steep slanting mountain slopes. Second, high elevation air is thinner than low elevation air. This reduces its ability to absorb heat from the ground.

The decrease in air temperature with increasing elevation also affects the moisture levels of the mountain environment. Warm moist air encounters mountainous terrain and is pushed upwards and cooled. Cool air can't hold as much suspended moisture as warm air, so the moisture falls out as rain and snow on mountain slopes. The cooler mountain air is also less effective at removing soil moisture through evaporation, leaving more in the ground for plant growth.

The combined effect of decreasing temperature and increasing moisture means mountain climates become cooler and moister the higher up we go. In the southern Appalachian Mountains which includes GSMNP, this provides progressively better plant growth environments up to about 4500 feet in elevation where cold winter temperatures, powerful prevailing winds, snow and ice limit the kinds and number of trees that can thrive there.

This elevation-related climate change can also be duplicated by traveling north. Driving 130 miles north produces about the same climate change as ascending 1000 feet in elevation. This explains why high elevation forests in GSMNP resemble those found many miles north in New England. Though similar, the Park's mountain forests are not an exact match of those to the north. There are some important differences that make southern Appalachian forests unique.

The lowest elevation in GSMNP is 875 feet above sea level and occurs along Abrams Creek in the extreme western part of the Park. At 6643 feet above sea level, Clingmans Dome is the highest point. It is also the third highest peak east of the Mississippi. But most of the land in GSMNP and the rest of the southern Appalachians ranges between about 1500 feet and 6500 feet. Ecologists divide this range into the following three mountain elevation zones.

Low elevation zone (1500 feet to 2500 feet)
Middle elevation zone (2500 feet to 4500 feet)
High elevation zone (4500 feet to 6500 + feet)

The map on page 13 shows the three elevation zones in the Park. **Be sure to go to the web site listed on page 3 to download full color versions of all the maps and graphs found in this book.** The elevation zone boundaries do not mark abrupt climate changes, but rather transition areas where progressively cooler and moister conditions eventually bring about significant changes in forest makeup.

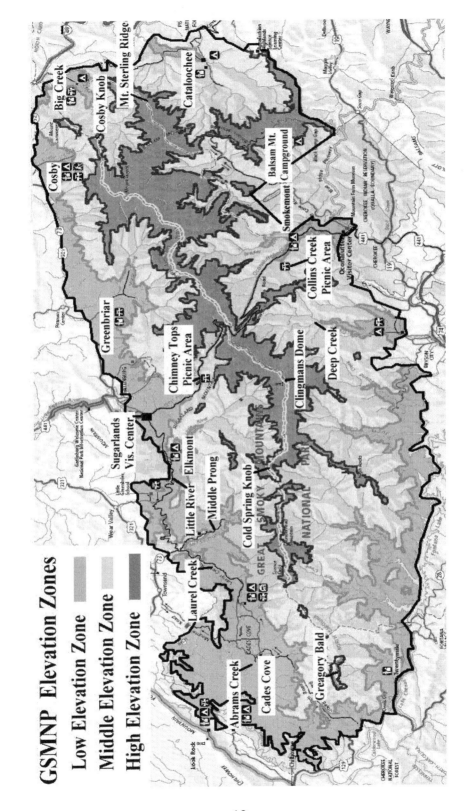

GSMNP Elevation Zones

Low Elevation Zone

Middle Elevation Zone

High Elevation Zone

Big Creek

Cosby Knob

Mt. Sterling Ridge

Cataloochee

Cosby

Balsam Mt.

Smokemont Campground

Collins Creek Picnic Area

Deep Creek

Greenbriar

Chimney Tops Picnic Area

Clingmans Dome

Sugarlands Vis. Center

Elkmont

Middle Prong

Little River

Cold Spring Knob

Laurel Creek

GREAT SMOKY MOUNTAINS NATIONAL PARK

Abrams Creek

Cades Cove

Gregory Bald

13

Low Elevation Zone (1500'-2500')

The low elevation zone covers roughly 25 percent of the Park's land area forming an irregular band around much of the Park's perimeter. All Park visitor centers, ranger stations, picnic areas (except Chimney Tops picnic area) and developed campgrounds (except Balsam Mountain campground) are situated within this zone. Highway 441 south of Collins Creek picnic area and north of the Chimney Tops picnic area crosses the low elevation zone as do virtually all other paved park roads. Significant stretches of all park rivers and many smaller streams flow through this zone as well.

The largest sections of low elevation zone land are found in the western part of the Park within the Abrams Creek drainage area (also called watershed) which includes Cades Cove, and in the lower watershed of the Little River including Middle Prong and Laurel Creek. In these areas, stream beds reside at around 1500 feet elevation and adjacent ridges seldom exceed 2500 feet. In most other low elevation areas of the Park, stream beds reside at or below about 2500 feet elevation and are surrounded by ridges rising a thousand feet higher, into the middle elevation zone.

Land in the low elevation zone has experienced more human disturbance than any other part of the Park. Forests here were cleared extensively for home sites, pastures and fields. Intensive agriculture exhausted the soil's natural fertility giving rise to soil erosion. Grazing farm animals almost eradicated the rich carpet of wildflowers, ferns and native grasses formerly abundant here. Eroding sediments filled streams, killing aquatic life. Early loggers built 'splash' dams to collect water for floating logs downstream. When released, the torrent of log laden water damaged stream channel structure. Later, full-scale corporate logging operations removed virtually all the remaining virgin forest (also called primary forest) in the low elevation zone; yet, a near century of forest re-growth in this prolific growing environment has done much to restore the land and rebuild the soil.

The human activities that wreaked havoc in the majestic forests also provided homes and food for the people of the mountains. Even the logging industry created jobs that helped mountain people live better. Today we know how to make a living from the land in less destructive ways, and we enjoy a prosperity that enables us to set aside special places like GSMNP so its mountain forests can continue to enrich people's lives for many generations.

A more recent and potentially greater threat to mountain forests than those described is the accidental introduction of pests from other countries and continents. These exotic pests thrive in American forests that have climates similar to their own, but lack the biological balances to keep them in check. They have proven lethal to American trees which have little or no resistance to their attacks. Their ravages have affected forests in all three elevation zones and will be discussed in detail in chapter 8. Forests in the low elevation zone have been heavily impacted by two of these pests. The chestnut blight wiped out the Park's American chestnut trees by the 1950's, and the hemlock wooly adelgid is currently killing Eastern hemlock trees throughout the Park and southern Appalachian Mountains.

The majority of low elevation land is located along rivers and large streams which support river cove forests where American sycamore and American hornbeam grow along with a variety of both lowland and mountain trees. Forests of Eastern hemlock often grow along creek flats in this zone with oaks and hickories on the slopes and protected ridgetops, and oak-pine forests on dry exposed ridgetops. Refer to the Master Plant List in the book's Appendix 2 for an alphabetical listing of major Park trees, including their Latin names.

Middle Elevation Zone (2500'-4500')
The middle elevation zone is the largest zone in the Park, comprising roughly 50 percent of the Park's half-million acres. Few roads traverse this zone. Highway 441 traverses it between the Collins Creek picnic area on the North Carolina side and the Chimney Tops picnic area on the Tennessee side, but by-and-large, the middle elevation zone is the domain of the horseman, hiker and backcountry camper. An extensive network of trails dotted with backcountry campsites crosses this zone providing access to the forest riches within.

Middle elevation zone land is found throughout the Park, but it is more abundant to the west of Highway 441 than to the east where high elevation land dominates. In the middle elevation zone the terrain becomes significantly steeper than down below. Stream size decreases and slopes become more rugged. Rich deep mountain coves are a characteristic feature of the middle elevation zone. Swift rocky streams course through the coves protected by ridges towering a thousand feet or more above.

Middle elevation land has had its share of human disturbance. Logging was the main culprit here, especially west of Highway 441. Removal of trees from steep slopes caused extensive soil erosion. The eroded soil found its way into streams, choking them with silt that wiped out the native brook trout and increased the frequency and severity of flash floods. Wildfires fed by huge piles of logging debris burned vegetation off steep slopes contributing to land slides that still scar some mountain flanks. The rich herbaceous layer of wildflowers, ferns and native grasses was less impacted here than down below where cultivation and grazing were extensive, but even so, logged forests here support only about half the kinds of herbaceous plants as do the Park's virgin forests.

Both chestnut blight and hemlock wooly adelgid have greatly affected forests in the middle elevation zone. These pests will be discussed further in the chapter on exotic tree pests.

Fortunately, the middle elevation zone still supports thousands of acres of virgin forest, such as those found on the upper watersheds of Deep Creek and Cataloochee Creek. These areas were protected from commercial logging by rough terrain or obstinate landowners unwilling to sell their timber. They contain some of the largest and oldest trees in the East, protected now from all but the ravages of exotic pests.

Middle elevation zone forests are the biological showcase forests of GSMNP and the southern Appalachians. Within this zone the temperature-moisture regime creates an ideal climate range for tree growth with cool temperatures and ample soil moisture. The mountainous terrain here provides a great variety of growing environments including deep fertile coves, creek flats, protected lower slopes, exposed upper slopes and exposed ridgetops. As a result, this zone possess the greatest diversity of tree species found anywhere in the eastern United States.

Along streams and in gaps the hiker passes through the classic cove hardwood forest (described later) where a characteristic mix of trees towers one hundred feet and more above a forest floor rich in colorful wildflowers.

Forests of hemlock often clothe steep protected slopes in the middle elevation zone, and the oak-hickory forests of exposed slopes are dominated by a mix of oaks different from those found lower down. Oak-pine forests on exposed slopes and ridgetops also reflect this altitude related change in tree mix.

High Elevation Zone (4500'-6643')

Land in this zone comprises roughly 20 percent of the Park's acreage. The high elevation zone dominates much of the ridge line separating Tennessee and North Carolina that forms the backbone of the Park. From about Cosby Knob in the northeast to Spence Field in the southwest, the high elevation zone follows the main divide in a wide continuous band branching off to encompass upper portions of several main ridges including Greenbrier Pinnacle, Hughes Ridge, Richland Mountain, Mt. LeConte, Thomas Ridge, Sugarland Mountain, Forney Ridge and Welch Ridge. Both northeast and southwest of this continuous band only the highest peaks are surrounded by islands of high elevation zone land, and southwest of Gregory Bald, the main divide drops permanently below the high elevation zone.

Mount Sterling Ridge in the northeast part of the Park runs south of, and parallel to the main divide, separating the Cataloochee and Big Creek watersheds. It connects with Balsam Mountain to form another large band of high elevation zone land. The Benton Mackaye Trail follows much of the ridge line here, providing access to this additional island of high country.

The high elevation zone of GSMNP is the true high country east of the Mississippi River, crested with many rugged peaks exceeding 5000 feet in elevation. The Appalachian Trail which follows the main divide is the major thoroughfare of travel here. Trails from lower down connect with it along its length providing rugged hiking and horseback access to this zone.

Highway 441 enters the high elevation zone briefly at Newfound Gap where it intersects the Appalachian Trail, and the Clingmans

Dome road parallels the Appalachian Trail from the gap to the dome.

Not even the high country escaped man's impact. In the early 1900's with gear-driven railroads, steam-powered log loaders and an army of men with saws and axes, the logging industry launched a successful campaign against much of the valuable spruce and fir timber abundant in this zone. Despite this mechanized onslaught, thousands of acres of virgin red spruce and northern hardwood forest remain, especially in the northeast part of the Park. Far more damaging than loggers, the balsam wooly adelgid discovered in the Park in 1963 has destroyed 90 percent of the mature Fraser firs there. Beginning in the early 1980's, Beech Bark Disease has done similar damage to the Park's rare beech gap forests.

If middle elevation forests are the biological showcase of the Park, high elevation forests are the scenic showcase, capturing the eye and imagination of the mountain traveler. A place of rugged exposed ridgetops, steep rocky ravines and shallow gaps, the high elevation zone presents a range of environments visually inspiring, but in which only a handful of tree species can thrive. Steep ravines support forests of red spruce, yellow birch and yellow buckeye with American beech on exposed slopes. Lower exposed ridgetops support forests of northern red oak while red spruce and Fraser fir occupy the highest exposed ridges and peaks.

CHAPTER 2. LANDFORM

Next to elevation, landform has the greatest influence on forests in GSMNP. Landform simply means the shape of the land. GSMNP has mountainous topography that creates a variety of places where forests can grow such as valleys, slopes and ridgetops. Each of these is called a landform. Topographic position is another name for landform. This variety of landforms enhances the richness and diversity of the forest types found there.

Landform influences accumulation and development of soil, the key ingredient in the flow of moisture and nutrients to the forest. A thick fertile layer of forest soil soaks up and holds water and dissolved nutrients like a sponge. Acting as a storage reservoir between rains, it provides plants with a continuous supply of these critical components. In areas where rich soil is abundant, trees prosper because they seldom experience the stress of prolonged drought. In turn, tree roots pull up nutrients from deep in the soil, redistributing them on the surface in the form of autumn leaves. The leaves decompose to form more compost-rich soil, continually improving the soil's moisture-storing ability. This is the legacy of the forest.

 Gravity removes soil and water from ridgetops and upper slopes, tending to make these environments dry and nutrient-poor. Conversely, soil and water accumulate on lower slopes and in valleys, making these environments moist and nutrient-rich. A mountain slope can be protected by adjacent slopes from hot summer sunshine, creating a cool moist environment favorable for plant growth. In the absence of a protecting adjacent slope the mountain's forested flank is exposed to hot summer sun resulting in a dryer less favorable environment.

Aspect refers to the compass direction a slope faces. Slopes that face generally south (south-facing aspect) receive significantly more sunlight during the year than those facing generally north. Slopes with south-facing aspects warm up earlier in spring, losing snow cover while their north-facing counterparts are still snow bound. They are hotter and dryer during the growing season and experience burning more often than north-facing slopes. This gives rise to thinner, less fertile soil and a forest composition often quite different from that of north-facing slopes.

The following paragraphs present and define the major landform types found in GSMNP. Each landform represents a less hospitable environment for trees than the previous type. Physical features like streams and ridges are also defined and categorized to make the idea of landform easier to apply to our study of the Park's forests. As you read about the Park's landforms, refer to the Google maps screen shot of the Smokement area on the next page that illustrates the landforms described. In the next chapter we give detailed instructions for accessing free topographic terrain maps of GSMNP from the internet and using them to interpret landform.

Stream Definitions

The Park's mountain streams contribute greatly to its pristine natural character, and they help create a variety of growing environments for trees. Every stream has its accompanying watershed that consists of all the acres of land whose waters (rain water and stream flow) drain into that particular stream. Drainage area is another name for watershed. We divide the Park's waters into three groups: rivers, prongs and creeks, loosely based on size and shape.

Rivers are the largest streams in the Park and are usually fringed with wide, flat areas of fertile land called bottomland. The Park's rivers are between 50 and 100 feet across and drain watersheds comprising at least 25,000 acres. To cross a river, I will likely have to swim. **Prongs** (also called forks) are narrower and steeper than rivers with less associated bottomland. Prong soils are generally less fertile and more acidic than river soils. Prongs are between 30 and 50 feet across and their watersheds comprise between 10,000 and 25,000 acres. I can usually wade across a prong. **Creeks** are the smallest streams in the Park. They generally lack bottomland. I can probably just jump across a creek! The above definitions sometimes contradict actual Park stream names. For example Abrams Creek is really a river-size stream along most of its course, but for the most part the Park's stream names correspond well with our definitions.

Coves

The word cove has long been used by mountain residents to describe a trough-shaped mountain valley usually traversed by a stream. We expand this definition to include valleys both wide and narrow where streams flow. Coves may face north (water flows generally north) or south (water flows generally south), and this affects the forests that grow there. In GSMNP coves are found along rivers, prongs and creeks.

River Coves

River coves are relatively wide valleys with areas of bottomland through which river-size streams flow. In the Park's low elevation zone (1500'-2500'), all its named rivers (Little River, W. Prong Pigeon River, Oconaluftee River, Little Pigeon River) form river coves. Raven Fork, Abrams Creek below Cades Cove, Big Creek and Cataloochee Creek also form river coves in the low elevation zone, because in this zone they are river-size streams.

Prong Coves
Prong coves are usually narrower, steeper, more acidic and less fertile than river coves with less associated bottomland, but they are larger than creeks. Prong coves in the Park's low elevation zone include lower Bradley Fork, Middle Prong of Little River, Laurel Creek, Abrams Creek (through Cades cove) and Rabbit Creek. Most other low elevation streams are creek-size.

In the middle elevation zone (2500'-4500') the Park's river coves become prong coves as they decrease in size with increasing elevation and slope, and prongs are generally reduced to creek-size streams. Above about 4500' ,only creeks are found, and above about 5000' creeks give way to steep dry ravines.

Coves present the most favorable growing conditions found in the mountains. The concave shape of the cove favors accumulation of fertile though sometimes acidic soil and provides protection from hot sun and cold wind as well as ample water for plant growth. We will see that river coves and prong coves can support different forest types and low elevation prong cove forests often differ from middle elevation prong cove forests.

Creek Flats, Draws, and Ravines
Creeks are smaller than prongs and are usually associated with flats. A creek flat (sometimes called a terrace) is a fairly narrow but relatively flat area paralleling the creek. The flat was carved out by the creek, but the creek has not accumulated deep, fertile soil deposits there as in the case of a river or prong.

Draws and ravines share the concave shape of creeks, but they possess no year-round flowing water. Draws typically become creeks as they descend the mountain, and they may become ravines as they ascend into higher elevation and become quite steep, narrow and shallow. Creek flats, draws and ravines are less favorable for tree growth than coves, but in GSMNP they can still support majestic forests quite often of hemlock and white pine.

Ridge Definitions

Ridges in the Park can be classified by their relationship to each other. The **main divide** is the high ridgeline that separates Tennessee and North Carolina and runs through the Park's center. A **main ridge** is a ridge branching from the main divide. Hughes Ridge and Sugarland Mountain are examples of main ridges. A **spur** ridge branches from a main ridge often roughly paralleling the main divide. Spur ridges usually don't have names. The Newton Bald Trail follows a spur ridge that branches from Thomas Divide, a main ridge.

Protected Slopes and Ridgetops

Protected mountain slopes are slopes on the mountain side that are shielded from hot sun and cold wind by adjacent taller slopes. Protected slopes are most abundant in the middle elevation zone, the largest zone in the Park. Here numerous high ridges protect each other's lower slopes from hot sun and cold wind. Ridgetops can also be protected, and many protected ridgetops exist on spur ridges in the Park where higher mountains surround and protect them. Protected slopes may face generally north (north-facing) or generally south (south-facing). As mentioned earlier, north-facing slopes are generally cooler and moister than south-facing slopes.

Exposed Slopes

Exposed slopes lack adjacent protecting ridges. They are exposed to the adverse effects of hot sun and cold wind. They are common in the Park's low elevation zone west of highway 441 where ridgetops rarely exceed 2500 feet elevation. They are also abundant in the high elevation zone where many ridgetops exceed 5000 feet in elevation. Exposed slopes may also face north or south.

Exposed Ridgetops

Exposed ridgetops are the least favorable environments for tree growth. Soil, water and nutrients are removed from these areas by gravity. Hot summer sun bakes the rocky soil and cold winter winds, snow and ice pound the exposed summits. Only hardy drought-tolerant trees survive well here.

CHAPTER 3. TOPOGRAPHIC MAPS
OF GREAT SMOKY MOUNTAINS NATIONAL PARK

Topographic maps possess the information needed for locating the forest types found in GSMNP. They tell you the elevation and landform of any forest location in the Park. You plug this information into the Forest Finder (introduced in the next chapter) to determine what kind of mature forest should grow there. This chapter tells how to find and print topographic maps of the Park.

The United States Geological Survey (USGS) has created topographic (topo) maps of most of the United States including the Smokies. You can download and print them from the internet simply for the cost of printer ink and paper. To save money, we suggest you print only the map you need for your immediate adventure, but do save a copy of each map in a folder on your computer for future use.

The Discover Life in America web site is the official GSMNP web site dedicated to discovering and documenting all lifeforms in the Park. You can access the USGS topo maps for the Park here at:

http://www.dlia.org/atbi/science/park_quad_pdfs/topo_index_24k.shtml

When you get there you'll find a window that looks like this:

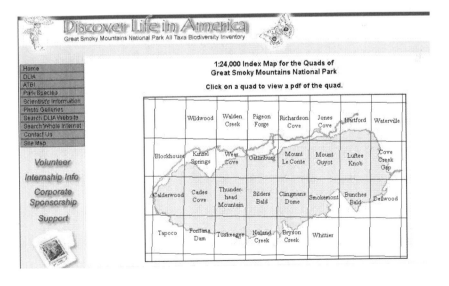

Just click on the rectangular area of interest to access the relevant topo map. The maps are displayed using Adobe Acrobat Reader, so you must have it installed on your computer. The installation is free and currently (2010) located at:

http://get.adobe.com/reader/

Google maps, another internet site, also has topo maps of GSMNP as well as the rest of the United States and much of the world. Google maps are excellent because they have a "terrain" feature that shows a three dimensional view of the terrain. Access Google Maps on the web at:

http://maps.google.com/

You will see a window that looks like this:

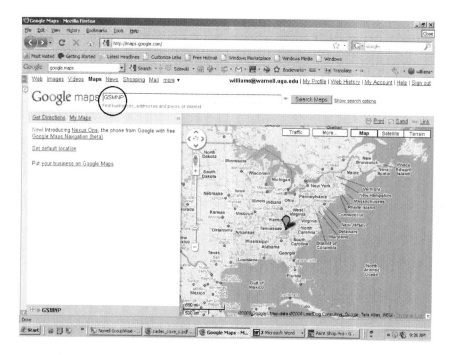

Type the letters GSMNP in the search maps text box and hit the enter key on your computer. Next you will get this window:

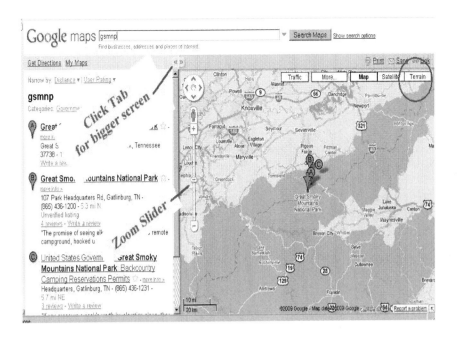

Click the tab shown above to get a bigger map screen. You can also hit the F-11 key on your keyboard to get a complete full screen view. Now hit the terrain button in the upper right corner of the window. Instead of the terrain button, you might see a button that says "More". Click there to find the terrain option. Use the zoom slider to get a close look at the terrain and contour lines of a particular location. Drag the map around with your mouse to find the particular location you seek.

Here is a Google maps screen shot of the vicinity of Smokemont campground in the Park. Be sure to visit the web site shown on page 3, and download a color version of this map section.

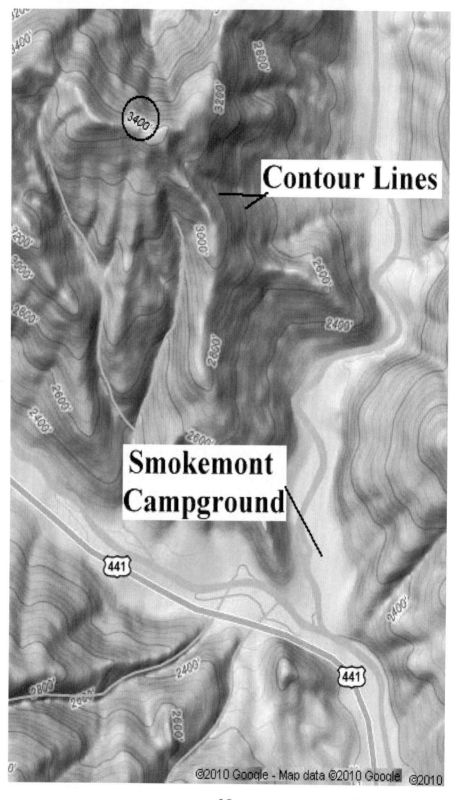

Contour Lines

Smokemont Campground

441

441

©2010 Google - Map data ©2010 Google ©2010

28

You can see the contour lines (brown on the full color map you can download, page 3) forming undulating lines on the map. The mountainous terrain is easily visualized with the 3-D terrain rendering. Highway 441 traverses the map as a labeled gray line. You can see the conjunction of the Oconaluftee River (on left) and the Bradley Fork (on right), both shown in blue on the color map download. Smokemont campground is not drawn in on the map, but it is located along the east side of Bradley fork at the stream conjunction.

The disadvantage of Google maps is some campgrounds and most of the hiking trails are not shown on these maps. This disadvantage can be overcome by using the official Park trail map obtainable on the GSMNP web site (and for $1.00 at Park visitor centers and campgrounds) in conjunction with the Google maps. Here is the web link:

http://www.nps.gov/grsm/planyourvisit/maps.htm

On USGS maps, Google topo maps and the official Park trail map the top of the map represents the compass direction, North. Measuring horizontal distance on the downloaded maps can be tricky because the map scale changes as you zoom and when the image is formatted for printing. Use the official Park trail map to determine trail distances. Its 3-D rendering will also assist you in transferring trail routes from the Park trail map to the Google topo maps you download and print.

The three-dimensional rendering of Google maps will help you learn to visualize terrain using contour lines on the map. This skill will come in handy when you view the USGS maps which lack the 3-D rendering.

Contour lines show the shape of the land by marking places on the ground located at a certain elevation above sea level. Notice the 3400-foot elevation contour line on the Smokemont map segment. Every point on that line is located at 3400 feet above sea level. Many contour lines, each representing a different elevation are shown on a topo map. Contour lines are equally spaced in terms of elevation. For example, the 3400-foot contour line and the 3200-foot contour line shown on the map segment are spaced at an elevation interval of 200 vertical feet. Lighter lines in between these are spaced at an interval of 40 vertical feet. The vertical spacing between contour lines is called the contour interval. Here are some additional brief guidelines for interpreting contour lines.

Contour lines show peaks or ridgetops by forming concentric circles.

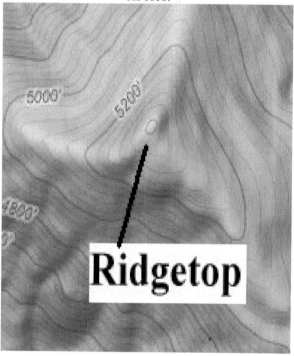

Contour lines form v-shapes where streams and valleys occur. The v shapes always point upstream.

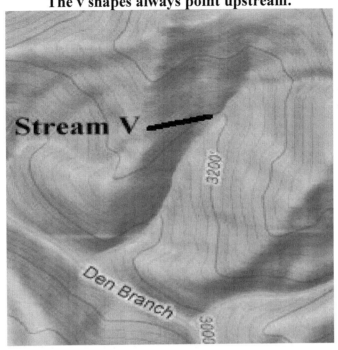

Closely spaced contour lines represent steep slopes.

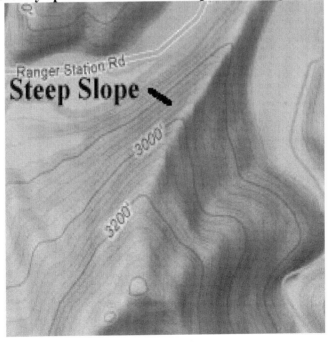

Widely spaced contour lines represent more gently sloping land.

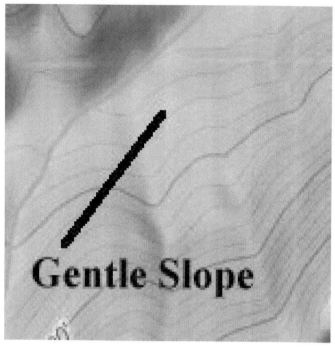

Printing Google Maps Screen Shots

Many readers know how to grab and print images from the web. Use what works for you. Here is a way that works on most computers with Windows operating system. Find the Google map section of the Park you want to print. Make sure the f-11 key is on so you have a full screen view. Now hit the *Print Screen* button on your keyboard. This puts a copy of the screen on the computer clipboard. Next open the Microsoft Paint program by hitting the following sequence on your computer:
Start
Programs
Accessories
Paint

In the Paint program hit *edit* then *paste.* This will create an image of the screen in the paint program. Now use the select tool to select the part of the map image you specifically want to print.

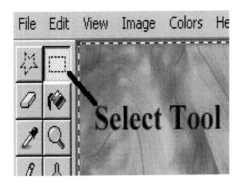

Next hit *edit* and then *copy*, and now *edit* and then *paste* to create an image of the selected area. Hit *file* and then *page setup* to select printing options. Finally hit *file print* to print the map, whew! Save the image to a map folder on your computer for future reference and printing. Remember the Google maps are owned by Google. Share them but don't sell them, so you won't be violating copyright laws. You are now ready to hit the woods or at least the next chapter!

CHAPTER 4. THE FOREST FINDER

When elevation and landform are considered together they provide a powerful tool for understanding the natural processes that created the magnificent forests found in GSMNP. In the next chapter we will account for much of man's impact in the Park by considering the third most important influence on forest composition, forest age, but first let's look at the Forest Finder, a visual tool for illustrating forest types found in the Park and throughout the southern Appalachian Mountains based on elevation and landform.

Important Note:
The description of the Forest Finder that follows refers to color-coded forest types. Please download color images, including the Forest Finder color version from the web site. It's free and easy to do! In the mean time grab some crayons and follow along!

http://www.forestsofgreatsmokymountains.com/

The vertical axis of the forest finder lists elevations from low to high, and its horizontal axis lists landforms from moist to dry. The major forest types of GSMNP are drawn on this graph as shaded areas, each in a different color. For example, cove forests are shaded in green. Within the green area several kinds of cove forests are labeled. As another example, northern red oak forests are shaded in red. Within the red area we find the northern red oak-hickory-red maple forest and the high elevation northern red oak forest. Later chapters in this book explain each forest type in detail.

The concept of representing GSMNP forest types in terms of elevation and landform was presented by R. H. Whittaker (Whittaker, R. H.) in his 1956 paper on the Park's forests. The Forest Finder is based on Whittaker's work. We have coined the term Forest Finder, and added color shading of forest types. We have also adjusted forest types to reflect ravages of the chestnut blight, the decrease in pine forests since Whittaker's day and to include insights gained from more recent research.

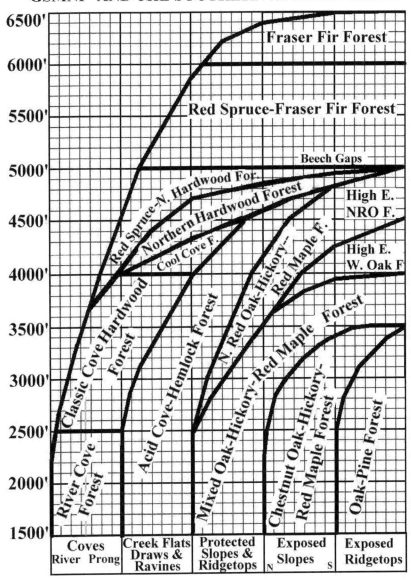

The Forest Finder is a condensed representation of the Park's forests. It combines the more than 50 detailed forest types, identified by researchers into fifteen more general forest types based on the most important trees found in each type. This author has spent considerable time identifying these fifteen forest types including many happy hours measuring over 120 non-invasive tree study plots in the Park. A working knowledge of the fifteen types gives you a mental framework that can form the basis for more detailed study, and for that we refer you to the excellent Discover Life web site (http://www.dlia.org/) and to the staff of dedicated and knowledgeable rangers, naturalists and volunteers who help preserve and interpret these wonderful forests.

The most visually striking aspect of the Forest Finder is the way the areas representing forest types lean or curve to the right as they project upwards. This shows how the temperature and moisture levels preferred by a particular forest type shift with increasing elevation. For example, the preferred temperature and moisture combination for Eastern hemlock is found along acidic creek flats at low elevations. In middle elevations, however, these same conditions are often found on steep protected slopes, so hemlock shifts with the habitat up on to protected slopes. This pattern stops in the high elevation zone because temperature overrides the influence of moisture. As a result, high elevation forest types dominate virtually all landforms within a given elevation range.

The Forest Finder depicts cove forests in green. Cove forests include river cove forests found along rivers and prongs in the low elevation zone. American sycamore and American hornbeam are diagnostic trees in this forest. The classic cove hardwood forest found along prongs and creeks in the middle elevation zone is characterized by a relatively large number of trees in the forest canopy (tree top level), a sparse understory (trees and shrubs below the canopy) and a very rich and diverse layer of wildflowers, ferns and grasses on the forest floor. The cool cove forest found in upper stream coves in the middle elevation zone, especially on the warmer North Carolina side of the main divide, is a transition forest between classic cove hardwoods and northern hardwoods. It lacks some important classic cove trees like yellow poplar, retains some like basswood and has more yellow birch and yellow buckeye, trees of the northern hardwood forest found higher up.

Acid cove-hemlock forests are outlined in purple on the Forest Finder. Eastern hemlock, an acid-loving tree, is the dominant tree in this forest. In younger forests of this kind, hemlock shares the forest canopy with yellow poplar, black birch and red maple on moist sites and with oaks and white pine on dryer sites. In older,

36

more mature forests, hemlock dominates the canopy exclusively. Rosebay rhododendron, an acid-loving shrub, is characteristic of the understory in this forest.

The mixed oak-hickory-red maple forest is shown in brown on the Forest Finder. Found on protected and exposed slopes in the low and middle elevation zones, this forest is characterized by a varying mix of oak trees including northern red oak, white oak, chestnut oak and scarlet oak. On cool moist sites northern red and white oaks predominate. Chestnut oak and scarlet oak dominate dryer, less fertile sites. Red maple is more prominent in most southern Appalachian oak forests today as a result of its role as a major replacement for American chestnut trees killed by the chestnut blight.

Orange is the color of the chestnut oak-hickory-red maple forest. Formerly the American chestnut-chestnut oak forest, it is now dominated by chestnut oak a major chestnut replacement on exposed slopes.

Oak-pine forests are depicted in gray. Pine forests, once abundant in the Park, are becoming less prominent with continued fire prevention and the advancing age of forests left undisturbed since the Park's inception in the early 1930's. On the driest ridgetops, pines like pitch pine and table-mountain pine will continue to dominate the forest. In less austere locations, deciduous trees like oaks and hickories will slowly replace pines like Virginia and shortleaf pines. During the past decade the National Park Service has instituted a prescribed burning policy aimed at restoring some of these forests to their pre-Park, pine-dominated state.

Northern red oak forests are shown in red on the Forest Finder. In the middle elevation zone the northern red oak-hickory-red maple forest dominates slopes. This too was once the realm of the American chestnut tree, and red maple has been a significant replacement tree here as well. On exposed ridgetops between 4500 and 5000 feet elevation, the high elevation northern red oak forest predominates. Northern red oak comprises at least 75% of the tree canopy in this chilly windswept ridgetop forest.

Oak forests dominated by white oak are depicted in pink. Though not abundant in GSMNP, the high elevation white oak forest is found on some exposed ridgetops in the 4000 to 4500 foot elevation range. Here a canopy of gnarled and stunted old white oaks characterizes this forest which is more common south of the Park where higher ridgetops average around 4000 feet.

Northern hardwood forests are shown in yellow on the Forest Finder. They dominate most landforms between 4500 and 5000 feet elevation. Three varieties are described. The red spruce-northern hardwood forest found extensively on the cool Tennessee side of the main divide is a transition forest between northern hardwoods and spruce-fir. The northern hardwood forest found more commonly on the North Carolina side and south of the geographic range of red spruce, lacks red spruce in its makeup which consists of yellow birch, yellow buckeye and formerly American beech, increasingly a victim of beech bark disease. Finally, the beech gap forest a very rare subtype of northern hardwood forest grows in pockets mainly on exposed slopes. This forest, once dominated by a canopy of stunted American beech trees, has also been devastated by beech bark disease and wild hogs that root out and destroy the rare herbs and sedges characteristic of the forest floor here.

The noble and picturesque spruce-fir forest drawn in dark blue on the Forest Finder dominates nearly all land forms between 5000 and 6000 feet elevation. Red spruce, Fraser fir and mountain ash are characteristic trees of this forest.

The Fraser fir forest in light blue dominates the highest ridges above 6000 feet in GSMNP. Today as you drive highway 441 across New Found Gap the stark gray crowns of dead virgin Fraser fir trees mark the surrounding slopes, the realm of this once majestic forest. Fraser fir, the dominant tree here, has been severely decimated by the balsam wooly adelgid.

The boundaries between forest types shown on the Forest Finder represent areas where adjacent forest types may mix. For example, on an exposed slope at 4700 feet elevation, you may find an acid cove-hemlock forest, a northern hardwood forest or a forest containing components of both types. Keep this in mind when you take to the woods to read the forest. Nature rarely presents us with ideal forest types. Her unpredictable nature, however, adds infinite variety and interest to her domain.

This book contains detailed descriptions of each forest type and Park locations where examples of each forest type may be observed. The reader will also find book sections describing the major trees and many shrubs of GSMNP. These descriptions won't replace a good field guide to tree identification, but they do provide information to help distinguish between tree look-a-likes and interesting tree facts not always found in the guides. The web site listed on page 3 contains a link to an image-based tree id web page describing all the trees listed in this book.

 The Forest Finder was created to help you plan your mountain adventures and to heighten the quality of your experience. You can determine what kind of forests you are likely to encounter on a hike, or you can target a particular forest type and visit locations where it grows. When you hike along a mountain trail, use the Forest Finder to determine the nature of the forest around you and understand the changes you see as you move through different forest habitats. As you become more familiar with the Park and its forests, you can modify the Forest Finder graph to reflect your own observations making it an even more useful tool and the basis for a rewarding and educational hobby.

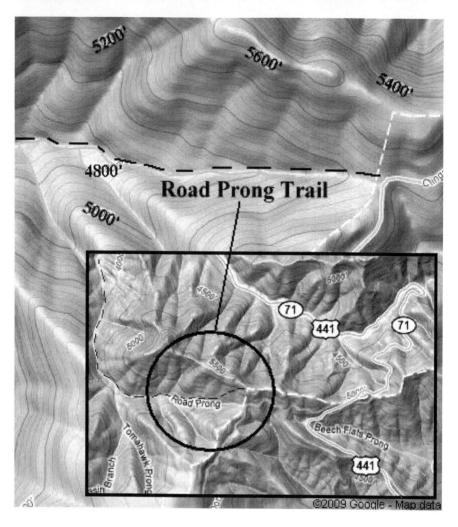

Let's look at an example that illustrates how to use the Forest Finder. I am planning to hike the Road Prong Trail from its intersection with the Clingmans Dome Road down to Highway 441 at the Chimney Tops parking lot. A glance at the topographic map of this area tells me the trail head is at about 5300 feet elevation. The map also shows the trail initially follows a dry ravine that becomes a creek at around 5000 feet.

On the Forest Finder I locate the 5300 foot elevation line and follow it over to the creek flats, draws and ravines landform. Looks like I will begin the hike in <u>spruce-fir forest</u> turning into <u>red spruce-northern hardwoods</u> as I descend. The descriptions of these forest types tell me I'll see red spruce, yellow birch and yellow buckeye in the mature canopy. I will read the descriptions of these trees so I can identify them there.

This is the cooler Tennessee side of the Park, so I may not find the cool cove forest here. Instead, below about 4000 feet as the trail descends along the stream, I should enter the <u>classic cove hardwood forest</u> where spruce is replaced by a mix of trees characteristic of this forest type, like basswood, silverbell, white ash and yellow poplar. I read up on these tree species in the chapter on trees, and will eagerly look for them as I descend the stream.

Great Smoky Mountains National Park
Forest Finder Forest Types

Low Elevation Zone (1500-2500')
- **Rivers**
  - **River Cove Forest**

- **Prongs**
  - **River Cove Forest**
  - **Acid Cove-Hemlock Forest**

- **Creek Flats, Draws and Ravines**
  - **Acid Cove-Hemlock Forest**
  - **Mixed Oak-Hickory-Red Maple Forest**

- **Protected Slopes and Ridgetops**
  - **Acid Cove-Hemlock Forest**
  - **Mixed Oak-Hickory-Red Maple Forest**

- **Exposed Slopes**
  - **Chestnut Oak Forest** (north-facing)
  - **Oak-Pine Forest** (south-facing)

- **Exposed Ridgetops**
  - **Oak-Pine Forest**

Middle Elevation Zone (2500-4500')

- **Prongs**
  - **Acid Cove-Hemlock Forest**
  - **Classic Cove Hardwood Forest**

- **Creek Flats, Draws and Ravines**
  - **Acid Cove-Hemlock Forest**
  - **Classic Cove Hardwood Forest**
  - **Cool Cove Forest** (4000'-4500', N.C. side)
  - **Red Spruce-Northern Hardwood Forest** (4000-4500', TN. side)

- **Protected Slopes and Ridgetops**
  - **Acid Cove-Hemlock Forest** (steep, north-facing)
  - **Mixed Oak-Hickory-Red Maple Forest** (south-facing)
  - **Northern Red Oak-Hickory-Red Maple Forest** (4000-4500')

- **Exposed Slopes**
  - **Chestnut Oak-Hickory-Red Maple Forest** (2500-3500')
  - **Mixed Oak-Hickory-Red Maple Forest** (3500-4000')
  - **Northern Red Oak-Hickory-Red Maple Forest** (4000-4500')

- **Exposed Ridgetops**
  - **Oak-Pine** (2500-3500')
  - **Chestnut Oak-Hickory-Red Maple Forest** (3000'-3500)
  - **High Elevation White Oak Forest** (4000-4500')

High Elevation Zone (4500-6600')

4500-5000'

- **Creek Flats, Draws and Ravines**
  Red Spruce-Northern Hardwood Forest
  (Tennessee Side)
  Northern Hardwood Forest

- **Protected Slopes and Ridgetops**
  Red Spruce-Northern Hardwood Forest
  (Tennessee Side)
  Northern Hardwoods Forest (N.C. Side)

- **Exposed Slopes**
  Northern Hardwood Forest
  Beech Gap Forest

- **Exposed Ridgetops**
  High Elevation Northern Red Oak Forest

5000-6600' All Landforms

Spruce-Fir Forest (5000-6000')

Fraser Fir Forest (6000-6600')

The information on elevation and landform found in the Forest Finder tells us what kind of mature forest we should expect to find when we visit, but there is more to the story of forest makeup. The next chapter addresses the formidable impact man's activities have had on the age of the forests in the Park.

CHAPTER 5. FOREST AGE

Next to elevation and landform, forest age has the greatest influence on forest composition in GSMNP. The term forest composition simply means the species of trees growing in the forest as well as the number and distribution of each species. A young forest is composed of a mix of tree species quite different from that of an older forest. The Forest Finder tells us what kind of mature forest ultimately develops on a particular site, but due to a variety of disturbances associated with the Park's history, we may not find a mature forest there.

The first settlers in what is now GSMNP encountered **virgin forests** (also called primary forests and original forests). Undisturbed by man for thousands of years, these virgin forests had long ago attained a mix of tree species we call climax. A **climax** forest is the stable end product of a long series of changes in forest composition over time. This series of changes is called **forest succession**, and most ecologists agree temperate forests require more than a century of forest succession to become climax forests. A young forest is just beginning the process of forest succession. An old forest has experienced several stages of forest succession, and may have achieved the status of climax forest.

So what is the difference between a virgin forest and a virgin climax forest? A virgin forest is any forest that has not been disturbed by man. A virgin climax forest is a virgin forest that has reached the ultimate successional stage of forest development called climax. Incidentally, the terms virgin and climax do sound a little strange, but they are the terms traditionally used by forest ecologists and interestingly, they accurately define the forests to which they refer.

Mature forests, including climax forests, contain several vertical growing environments that trees may occupy, and trees can be classified based on their preferred vertical position. **Dominant canopy** trees like yellow poplar and white oak occupy the highest vertical position in the forest-- the canopy-- where they receive abundant sunlight. Typically, two or three tree species dominate the canopy in large numbers. **Dispersed canopy** trees like black cherry and white ash share the canopy with the dominants, but in fewer numbers and they are usually more dispersed throughout the forest. Both dominant and dispersed canopy trees can occupy lower vertical levels as they grow toward the canopy. **Subcanopy** trees like sourwood and American holly reside just below the canopy dominants, and **understory** trees like dogwood and hornbeam live in the shade below the subcanopy. Subcanopy and understory trees don't move into the canopy. They are permanently adapted to the positions they occupy.

Settlers cut the original forests they found and in the process turned the succession clock back to time zero (bare ground). They held the clock at time zero by maintaining open areas as home sites, fields and pastures. The logging industry also turned back the succession clock, but left thousands of tree stumps capable of sprouting into a forest more quickly than one starting from bare ground. After farming and logging ceased in the Park around 1934, new forests began to grow. Forest succession commenced.

The following paragraphs describe five forests that help illustrate the stages of forest succession as they occur in the southern Appalachian Mountains. Today we find all five stages of forests in GSMNP. It is important to note that the time required for each stage varies depending on site characteristics and past history, so when you read the time span listed for each successional stage, mentally put the word, "about" in front.

The Developing Forest (0-50 years)
Forest succession begins when **pioneer** trees like pine, black locust, cherries and yellow poplar colonize abandoned land or re-sprout from logged land. Like the tough and enduring pioneers who first settled these forests, pioneer trees are a special breed adapted to the often harsh conditions found on abandoned, worn out land. Pioneer trees require the full sunlight found on open sites to survive and grow, and they are called **shade-intolerant** trees for this reason.

Pioneer trees grow relatively fast. By about age 15 years their young crowns have grown together creating a closed, low canopy. The forest is quite dense with many small trees per acre composed of only a few different tree species, the vast majority of which are pioneer trees.

As the developing forest grows, changes occur. The pioneer trees grow taller reaching mature height by about age 50 years. During this time fierce competition for sunlight, water and nutrients has thinned the ranks of the developing forest creating a more open understory. Pioneer tree root systems have broken up the soil and brought new nutrients and organic matter to the soil surface in the form of autumn leaves. Conditions of soil moisture and fertility are better than they were in the beginning, but not enough sunlight penetrates the canopy to support the sun-loving seedlings of pioneer trees. This ushers in the next stage of forest succession.

Pioneer Forest (50-100 years)
Pioneer trees continue to dominate the canopy of the pioneer forest, but another group of trees called **shade-intermediate** trees begins to take dominance from the pioneers. Trees like oak, birch and red maple have become established as seedlings under the shade of pioneer trees, but they need the sunlight of forest openings to mature and grow into the forest canopy. Openings are provided by the death of pioneer trees due to competition, disease, flood, fire, wind and ice. Shade-intermediate trees take advantage of the openings growing into the canopy where they will eventually replace the pioneers.

This process occurs over the next 50 years as most of the short-lived pioneer trees die of old age. Yellow poplar, one of the few long-lived pioneer trees is an exception. A handful of poplars will remain to become giant monarchs in the old forest to come. After about 100 years, most of the forest canopy trees are shade intermediates with a few pioneer trees comprising the balance. The trees are fewer in number now, but average tree diameter is greater.

Intermediate Forest (100-200 years)
Trees intermediate in shade tolerance dominate the canopy during this stage, but another final wave of new trees slowly wrests dominance from them. **Shade-tolerant** trees like hemlock, beech, sugar maple, buckeye and hickory become established as seedlings in the full shade of the forest floor. They can grow to maturity in

the limited sunlight of the understory, though they do take advantage of openings not claimed by the faster growing intermediate trees. The slowest growers, and the longest lived members of the tree world, shade-tolerant trees may remain in the understory for 100 years eventually rising into the canopy to share dominance with trees already there.

By now the forest has established a well developed subcanopy layer and an understory layer where trees specifically adapted to these environments grow, and where future canopy trees waiting for new openings bide their time. In addition, the soil has become deeper and more fertile as a result of the forest building process.

Mature Forest (200-250 years)
By age 200, shade tolerant trees equal or exceed intermediate trees in the forest canopy. Shade tolerant trees will dominate the forest canopy from now on accompanied by a few intermediates and one or two old yellow poplars. The number of trees per acre has greatly declined as pioneer and intermediate trees have succumbed to competition and old age, but average tree size has increased considerably with many in the 30-inch plus diameter range. By now the forest floor has developed a thick layer of humus-rich soil that supports a flourishing non-woody plant community.

Climax Forest (250 + years)
The climax forest is the ultimate expression of forest development. Old age and the struggle for survival have greatly thinned the climax forest, but the remaining trees are quite large and show signs of advanced age like lichen encrusted bark, dead limbs in the canopy, hollow trunks and lightening blasted tops. When the ancient giants fall their root masses come out of the ground leaving pits. When these root masses decay creating mounds, a pit and mound topography develops that is characteristic of the climax forest as is the abundance of decaying logs on the forest floor.

Openings created in the climax forest by natural disturbances let sunlight down into lower levels where forest succession begins anew. Small openings created by the death of one or two trees are usually filled by intermediate trees because they can grow into the gaps faster than shade tolerant trees. Medium sized gaps like those created by wind and ice allow enough space for shade tolerant trees to move up along with the intermediates. Large openings like those created by fire, drought and disease favor pioneer trees by providing plenty of sunlight for pioneer tree seedling establishment and growth. Over time this creates a patchwork of mostly ancient forest interspersed with patches of younger trees of various ages. This multiple-age structure is the hallmark of the climax forest.

All virgin forests in the Park are climax forests. They reached the climax stage of forest succession with no interference from man and have existed as climax forests undisturbed for many centuries. Though definitions vary, the term **old-growth forest** usually refers to a climax forest that may have experienced limited disturbance by man such as firewood harvest, repeated understory burning or cattle grazing. A **second-growth forest** is one that has developed on land formerly cleared by man. Old growth and second-growth forests lack the biological diversity of their virgin forest counterparts.

Virgin climax forests are especially rich in herbaceous plants specifically adapted to grow there. Spring ephemerals (wildflowers that complete their entire above-ground life cycle in early spring before canopy foliage appears) include trout lily, toothwort, spring beauty, Dutchman's breeches and lady's-slippers. Another group of early spring wildflowers including bloodroot, windflower, hepatica, crested dwarf iris and trilliums retain leaves after their early spring flowers have disappeared. Representing still another survival strategy, evergreen plants like wild ginger, partridge-berry and galax are able to make food from the sun's energy (photosynthesize) year-round on the shady forest floor. Plants that are parasitic on the roots of trees also thrive in the shade. Squaw root, beech drops and Indian pipes, all devoid of chlorophyll, flourish at the base of their host trees.

The numerous canopy openings in the climax forest allow sunlight to filter down to the forest floor in places where a rich display of shade-intermediate herbaceous plants thrive. Dolls-eyes, blue cohosh, white snakeroot and intermediate woodfern are but a few of the beauties encountered on a hike through the virgin classic cove hardwood forest.

The Tree Table, Appendix 1. lists the major trees found in GSMNP forests, their shade tolerance ratings and the preferred vertical niche of each tree. The table also shows moisture preferences for GSMNP trees. This information is important because tree types involved in forest succession vary depending on site moisture characteristics. Each major temperature-moisture regime has its suite of pioneer, intermediate and shade tolerant trees that participate in forest succession there. For example, pines (except white pine) are the shade-intolerant pioneer trees on dry sites, whereas yellow poplar and black locust fill this role on more moist sites. The Forest Finder graphically illustrates this fact.

Reading The Forest

A basic knowledge of tree identification is necessary to understand succession in these magnificent forests. Please do not be daunted by this challenge! A good way to begin is to become familiar with the shade intermediate canopy trees from the Tree Table (page 235). American sycamore, an important intermediate tree in river cove forests is easily recognized by its stark white, apparently barkless upper trunk. Red maple, a common intermediate tree on both moist and dry sites has leaves and twigs arranged in opposite pairs, a good identification characteristic even in winter. All birches have distinctive bark patterns. On slopes below 5,000 feet elevation, oaks are the most important intermediate trees. They are fairly easily recognized as a group, and group recognition is usually enough to determine successional stage.

With a basic working knowledge of the shade intermediate canopy trees you will be well on your way to determining the successional stage of the forest that surrounds you. This skill will open a door of understanding and appreciation of the natural world that will enrich your life. There are many excellent tree identification guides. Tree Of The Smokies by Steve Kemp and Native Trees of the Southeast by L. Katherine Kirkman, Claud L. Brown and Donald J. Leopold are two we recommend. A Field Guide To The Trees And Shrubs Of The Southern Appalachians by R. E. Swanson is another great tree id reference. Also the Virginia Tech. Dendrology web site is a great source of tree id information:

http://www.cnr.vt.edu/DENDRO/DENDROLOGY/main.htm

As previously mentioned, the Forest Finder tells us the kind of <u>mature</u> forest to expect on a particular site. Now let's learn to tell if forests we encounter have reached the mature stage or if they exist in an earlier or later stage of forest succession.

To determine successional stage begin by identifying the canopy trees (both dominant and dispersed canopy). They are the tallest trees on the site. Their crowns form a closed canopy intercepting most of the sunlight. Usually two or three tree species dominate the canopy with relatively large numbers of each species. Next, check the Tree Table to determine if the canopy trees are pioneer trees, intermediate trees, shade tolerant trees or some combination. From this point, the process is straightforward.

A developing forest is easy to spot. Look for a thick stand of young pioneer trees of mostly 1 or 2 tree species. The trees haven't reached mature tree height yet (about 50 feet) and the understory is low with little sunlight penetrating to the forest floor. The developing forest is usually less than 50 years old. In GSMNP, yellow poplar is a very common tree in developing forests on moist sites. Black locust and white pine are common on dryer sites.

If pioneer trees dominate a canopy that has reached mature height, the forest is a pioneer forest probably between 50 and 100 years old. Shade intermediates will be in the subcanopy and understory waiting for openings they can claim.

If the canopy dominants are mostly shade intermediates with a mixture of pioneers and shade tolerants comprising the balance, the forest is an intermediate forest, probably between about 100 and 200 years old. The subcanopy and understory are well developed with trees (for example, sourwood and dogwood) especially adapted to the space below the canopy. Shade tolerant trees biding their time will also occupy these lower layers.

If big shade tolerant trees equal or exceed the intermediates you are likely looking at a mature forest 200-250 years old. The trees are well spaced and large, in the 30-inch plus diameter range.

Understory layers are well developed and the herbaceous layer is often species rich.

Climax forests (250 years+) are recognized by the signs of advanced age mentioned earlier. Wherever virgin forests are found in the Park they are climax forests. Look for the pit-and-mound topography, abundant dead tree trunks on the forest floor and the presence of forest openings in earlier stages of succession. Be careful, though. Pit-and-mound topography is also found in younger forests regenerating from former virgin forests that were logged but not farmed.

If the largest diameter trees on the site are not the **dominant** canopy trees, the forest is probably of two different ages a common occurrence in the Park. Old shade trees on abandoned home sites, trees along former roads and trees adjacent to stream channels are often much older than the surrounding forest. In many locations the logging industry left a few trees standing. Large intermediate or shade tolerant trees in the dispersed canopy are likely trees considered too small or malformed for the logger's saw back then that have grown to be the largest trees in the forest today.

These large (30+ inches in diameter) intermediate or shade tolerant trees are out of successional place when compared with the smaller dominant canopy trees that represent a younger forest growing up around them. Keep in mind the tendency of yellow poplar, a pioneer tree to remain into the climax forest stage. Very large yellow poplars surrounded by a dominant canopy of much smaller and more numerous yellow poplars also usually denote a stand of two different ages. Use the tree table to determine the successional stage and associated age range of these older trees.

Estimating Tree Age

Shade intolerant pioneer trees are the first trees to reach and hold the forest canopy when a new forest develops whether from bare ground or sprouting stumps. Consequently they are usually the oldest trees in the forest. Enjoying the benefits of full sunlight, they grow rapidly and at a fairly consistent average growth rate that declines gradually with age. This means we can use the diameter of the average size pioneer **canopy** trees on a site as a rough estimator of forest age. Shade intermediate and shade tolerant trees don't normally provide as accurate age information because they may spend 100 years as suppressed subcanopy trees with negligible diameter growth during that time.

The table below shows simple equations for estimating the age of yellow poplar trees from tree diameter at breast height (dbh). By the way, foresters and ecologists consider breast height to be 4 feet 6 inches above the ground. The equations are based on diameter and age data for southern Appalachian yellow poplar in second growth natural stands on sites of moderate moisture and fertility. The data were broken into diameter ranges and simple linear regression performed on each range. Regression equations were then simplified.

Yellow Poplar Diameter Range	Equation To Estimate Age
0-13"	Age = 5 X Diameter/2
14-16"	Age = 5 X Diameter-30 years
17-19"	Age = 5 X Diameter-20 years
20-30"	Age = 5 X Diameter

Virginia pine, black locust and black cherry are also shade intolerant pioneer trees found in the Park. The table below contains equations for estimating age from the diameter of these trees. The equations for Virginia pine and black locust are based on the yellow poplar equations since their growth patterns are similar.

Tree Species	Equation To Estimate Age
Virginia Pine	Yellow Poplar Age + 10 years
Black Locust	Yellow Poplar Age + 12 years
Black Cherry	Age = 9 X Diameter - 30 years

Let's take as an example a tree with a diameter of 10 inches dbh. A 10-inch yellow poplar's age would be estimated as 5 times diameter divided by 2, or 25 years old. A 10-inch Virginia pine would be 25 +10 or 35 years old. A 10-inch black locust would be 25+12 or 37 years old and a 10-inch black cherry would be 9 times 10 minus 30 or 60 years old.

Use these age equations by averaging the diameters of the largest canopy pioneer trees in the forest stand, and then calculating age from this average. Remember they provide only rough age estimates and should be used to reinforce your conclusions based on forest composition. When they disagree with more accurate information, discard them.

Red maple, a shade intermediate tree is very common in the southern Appalachians growing in most low and middle elevation forest types found in the Park. The table below presents diameter-based age estimation equations for red maple derived like those for yellow poplar. Consider them less reliable than those for yellow poplar, and so use them with caution.

Red Maple Diameter Range	Equation To Estimate Age
0-5"	$Age = 6 \times Diameter - 10$ years
6-12"	$Age = 6 \times Diameter - 20$ years
13-18"	$Age = 6 \times Diameter - 30$ years
19-20"	$Age = 6 \times Diameter - 20$ years
21-25"	$Age = 6 \times Diameter$

Unlike most shade tolerant trees, Eastern hemlock, a tree common in the Park (so far), demonstrates fairly consistent diameter growth over time. A good but rough age estimate can be calculated simply by multiplying its diameter times 10.

It's important to remember the diameter-age equations refer to forest-grown trees, not to open-grown trees. Open-grown trees are easily recognized by their wide spreading crowns and large branches low down on the trunk, indicators of the open sunny environments in which they once grew. Open-grown trees like those in pastures or along roads grow much faster than forest-grown trees.

It's also important to remember that the age equations presented become less accurate for trees greater than 30 inches in diameter. For example, if you find a 40-inch dbh hemlock, you know it is quite old, but probably not 400 years old-- the age predicted by its associated age equation (10 times dbh).

Based on the equations above, any forest-grown tree you encounter in GSMNP with a dbh greater than 30 inches is very likely to be over 100 years old. This makes sense because yellow poplar is one of the fastest growing trees in the Park, and a 30-inch forest grown poplar is around 150 years old. Virtually all other trees grow more slowly than poplar, so 30-inch specimens of other species are likely to be at least 150 years old. This fact is useful for identifying trees that predate both corporate logging and the land abandonment associated with the Park's establishment. As mentioned earlier they are often mixed in with younger trees in the forests of GSMNP.

The next chapter looks at how past disturbances caused by farming and corporate logging have effected forest makeup in GSMNP.

CHAPTER 6. DISTURBANCE BASED FOREST GROUPS IN GSMNP

Knowledge of the past history of a forest site can give excellent information about the age of the existing forest there, and fortunately information of this kind is available for the Park from the work of researcher Charlotte Pyle (Pyle, Charlotte). Existing forests in GSMNP can be classed in four groups based on the kind of past disturbance each group experienced. The disturbance history of each group gives us important clues to the age and successional stage of the forests found there today.

The four groups listed in order of decreasing acreage are, **post-logging forests, post-settlement forests, virgin forests and disturbed old-growth forests**. These forest areas are shown in several colors on the map you can download from our web site, and we hope you will do just that. It's free! The black and white version follows.

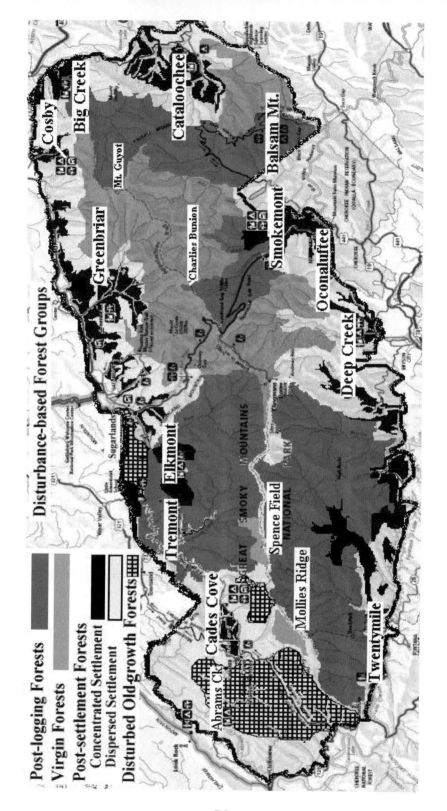

Post-logging Forests

Virgin Forests

Post-settlement Forests
Concentrated Settlement
Dispersed Settlement

Disturbed Old-growth Forests

Disturbance-based Forest Groups

Cosby

Big Creek

Cataloochee

Balsam Mt.

Mt. Guyot

Greenbriar

Charlies Bunion

Smokemont

Oconaluftee

Deep Creek

Sugarlands

Tremont

Elkmont

GREAT   SMOKY   MOUNTAINS

Spence Field

NATIONAL   PARK

Mollies Ridge

Cades Cove

Abrams Ck.

Twentymile

Post-logging Forests (medium gray)

The corporate logging era began around 1900 when big logging companies bought land in the Smokies and commenced large-scale industrial logging operations. When they were finished, 40 % of the present Park's acreage had been clearcut. Logging company officials had become wealthy in the process, and local mountain communities had received jobs, schools, churches, transportation systems and medical facilities. Many people benefited, but the environmental price tag was horrendous.

The term clearcut means to cut all useable trees in an area. Loggers typically cut all desirable trees larger than 10-15 inches diameter for lumber. Desirable lumber trees included yellow poplar, cucumbertree, American chestnut, basswood, maple, oak, white pine, birch, yellow pine, ash and silverbell. Smaller trees were cut for pulpwood, the raw material of the paper-making industry. In addition, logging towns like Tremont, Elkmont and Smokemont, housing hundreds of company employees consumed huge quantities of firewood for cooking, washing and home heating. When the company pulled out of an area, it left only a few standing trees amidst a vast army of stumps.

Today's forest industry has learned respect for the land that supports it. Environmental ethics are incorporated into forest management policies as well as the laws that regulate the industry. Best management practices that minimize soil erosion, enhance wildlife values and ensure protection of stream water quality form an essential legal and ethical basis for the growing and harvesting of trees. Places of outstanding natural character like GSMNP are now set aside, never to see the flash of the saw or hear the ring of the logger's axe again. The value of these preserved forests far surpasses the material wealth that might be derived from the harvest of timber.

Location	Logging Company	Appx. Dates Logged	Appx. Present-day Forest Age Range In Yrs.
W. Prong Little River	Little R. Lumber Co.	1903-1908	100-106
Little R., main or east fork (Elkmont)	Little R. Lumber Co.	1905-1926	83-104
Middle Prong Little River, (Tremont)	Little R. Lumber Co.	1926-1939	70-83
Hazel Ck.	Ritter Lumber Co.	1907-1928	81-102
Noland & Forney Cks.	Norwood Lumber Co.	1909-1920	90-101
Oconaluftee River, (Smokemont)	Three M and Champion Fiber Co.	1900-1934	75-109
Balsam Mountain	Whitmer-Parsons Lumber Co.	?	
Big Creek	Crestmont Lumber Co.	1908-1918	91-101

LOGGING TABLE

Most of the watershed of the Little River (Tremont and Elkmont area) was cut by the Little River Lumber Company owned by Col. W. B. Townsend, for whom the village of Townsend, Tennessee is named. The logging table above, shows that West Prong of Little River was the first area cut by the company between 1903 and 1908. Next came the main channel of Little River between 1905 and 1926. Middle Prong of Little River was the last area cut by Little River Lumber Company between 1926 and 1939, and the last area ever to be logged in the Park.

On the opposite side of the main divide in North Carolina, the William M. Ritter Lumber company cut Hazel Creek watershed from 1907 to 1928 feeding lumber and pulp mills that were part of a massive corporate enterprise later absorbed by the Georgia-Pacific Corporation. Noland and Forney Creeks were cut around the same time by the Norwood Lumber Company. These two areas contain the largest contiguous chunk of post-logging forest in the Park.

Northeast of 441, the Big Creek watershed was logged between 1908 and 1918 by Crestmont Lumber Company. Just across Balsam Mountain to the south, about the same time, the Whitmer-Parsons Pulp and Lumber Company was logging Straight Fork watershed and the land surrounding the Balsam Mountain Road, a former logging railway. These two areas form the second largest chunk of post-logging forest in the Park.

A smaller section of post-logging forest covers the watershed of Oconaluftee River and Lower Bradley Fork. As you travel 441 from Smokemont toward Newfound Gap, post-logging forest surrounds you until you reach Thomas Ridge at the second switchback. From there, virgin forest is on your left with post-logging forest on the right.

The smallest post-logging forest (not shown on map) consists of the watershed of Hesse Creek in the western part of the Park, northwest of Cades Cove.

The logging table shows that post-logging forests in the Park are between about 70 and 109 years old now. This would place them in the late pioneer or early intermediate stage of forest succession.

We would expect trees with intermediate shade tolerance ratings to dominate the canopy in most of these forests. Sycamore, black and yellow birch, red maple, and white ash would dominate moist sites like coves. Oaks and some white pine would dominate the slopes and ridgetops.

At this stage we might expect to see shade intolerant pioneer trees comprising most of the remainder of the canopy along with a few shade tolerant trees as well. Yellow poplar would definitely be present on moist sites like coves, creek flats and low protected slopes and likely be the biggest tree in the stand at around 19 to 22 inches in diameter. It would be accompanied by black cherry (11-16") and perhaps cucumbertree. Black locust (16-19"), sassafras, shortleaf pine, Virginia pine (17-20") and pitch pine would be the shade intolerant pioneer trees found on dryer sites like exposed slopes and ridgetops where dry conditions, possibly in conjunction with fire, slow the process of forest succession. These forests are likely to be pioneer forests instead of intermediate forests.

On moist middle elevation sites (classic cove hardwood forest) basswood, a fairly fast growing shade tolerant tree would likely be in the dispersed canopy in intermediate forests. On dryer sites, a hickory or two might be there, but most of the shade tolerant trees would still be in the subcanopy and understory waiting for openings and growing very slowly in the meantime with buckeye, sugar maple and hemlock on moist sites, and beech, silverbell and hickory in dryer conditions.

As an example of a post-logging forest, consider a site along the Middle Prong of Little River near Tremont, at about 1800' elevation. The Forest Finder indicates a low elevation river cove forest or an acid cove-hemlock forest should grow here, and the logging table shows this forest should be around 75 years old. On the site we find yellow poplar, sycamore, black birch and red maple dominating the canopy. This fits our expectation of mostly shade-intermediate trees in dominance along with a few pioneers. The canopy poplars average around 19 inches in diameter. Applying the age equation for yellow poplar gives an age of around 75 years (19 x 5-20). Hemlock and red maple dominate the subcanopy with American hornbeam and dogwood comprising the understory on this low elevation river cove site.

Not far from here, big (over 30 inches) silverbells and bitternut hickories, both shade tolerant trees, dominate the canopy with much smaller red maples and birches in the subcanopy. What happened here? Most likely the big shade tolerant trees, part of a mature forest, were somehow missed by loggers. A younger forest is growing up around them. This is a common situation in the Park. Be prepared for interesting exceptions to the model. Nature and man in league have created quite a mosaic!

Post-settlement Forests

About 22 % of the Park's land supports forests regenerating from former settlements. Areas of concentrated settlement are shown in black on the map. They occupy virtually all major rivers and prongs in the low elevation zone. Here buildings, agricultural fields, pastures and woodlots were numerous and closely spaced. Dispersed settlement areas (depicted in light gray) had more widely spaced farms and experienced some small-scale logging or regular burning. They are also mainly restricted to the low elevation zone.

The Cades Cove and Cataloochee districts contain large sections of concentrated post-settlement forests. Both districts were heavily settled with Cataloochee having supported the largest community located in the present Park. As with other post-settlement forests, these forests originated when the National Park Service purchased private farmland for incorporation into the Park, an ongoing process, mostly completed by 1934 with the Park's official designation. That would make them roughly 80 years old today.

Unlike post-logging forests that have regenerated fairly rapidly from stump sprouts, post-settlement forests have by-and-large regenerated from seeds blown into former fields and pastures containing soils depleted of nutrients and moisture-holding capacity by past agricultural practices. Though approximate contemporaries of their post-logging counterparts, they have often experienced forest succession at a slower pace. Abandoned fields support a thick growth of nearly pure yellow poplar, black locust or white pine with little understory. Termed early successional forests by some researchers, they stay in the pioneer forest stage longer than average, slowly repairing the soil so intermediate and shade tolerant trees can become established.

Exotic invasive plants (plants from other regions or countries) are more common in post-settlement forests than in other forests. Settlers planted many exotic ornamental and fruit trees around their homes. Common exotic invasive trees found in the Park include mimosa, tree-of-heaven, princesstree, Norway spruce and white poplar. Shrubs include autumn-olive and Chinese privet. Many non-native herbaceous plants grow on former settlement sites. It is not unusual to see daffodils and daylilies sprouting up around stone piles in the midst of the forest. Former home sites, these grounds were once lovingly tended by folks who lived, loved and died nearby. They are gone, but their flowers remain, forming a link between hearts and minds that spans the gap of time.

Cultural artifacts are good clues for interpreting the history of post-settlement forests reclaiming abandoned farm land. A lone chimney (chimney fall) reveals a former home site. We envision a mountain cabin surrounded by a few giant old open-grown trees. There must be an old roadbed nearby leading to the cabin and beyond. Its track may be lined with large trees older than the surrounding forest. It could be the trail we hiked to get here. Our mountain family probably grew corn and other crops on the most level land in the vicinity, and we look for piles of stones plucked from the fields and hauled to its edges. On steeper terrain, nearby remnants of wire fencing reveal a former pasture where cows grazed among widely spaced open-grown oaks, some of which remain surrounded by younger forest. In a former woodlot where the mountain family obtained fire wood we might expect to see large oak trees forked about waist high, testimony to the firewood cutter's axe and the vigorous sprouting tendency of oaks.

Cataloochee Creek provides good examples of concentrated post-settlement forests. Valley bottomland residing at about 2500 feet elevation once clothed with river cove and acid cove-hemlock forests, was cleared for agriculture by settlers in the early 1800s. A variety of crops including corn, wheat, beans and white potatoes planted in rich flat bottomland fields produced ample food for valley residences. The large barns left standing in the valley by the Park Service attest to abundant harvests experienced in this secluded realm where a good life could be had for the price of hard work.

Settlers also cleared adjacent slopes up to about 2700' elevation. Here they established apple orchards and pastures for livestock. Much of the forest land above 2700 feet elevation, however, was left fairly undisturbed, allowed to remain as virgin acid cove-hemlock forest and virgin classic cove hardwood forest.

Notwithstanding the valley's prosperity, cemeteries on the hills overlooking Cataloochee testify that many of its children died before the age of 5 years. Several gravestones also remind visitors of the toll taken by the deadly influenza epidemic of the World War I era. The cemeteries provide a snapshot of life in a time before the advent of the lifesaving medicines and disease prevention techniques we take for granted today.

With the Park's establishment in the early 1930's Cataloochee's farms were abandoned. The Park Service burned most of the buildings, leaving a few houses and barns to interpret the Valley's agrarian lifestyle. Much of the flat open bottomland along the creek has been maintained as pasture for the growing population of elk reintroduced into the area by the Park Service. On other former fields abandoned since the Park's inception, thick early succession forests of yellow poplar and white pine have become established. After about 80 years these forests are still in the pioneer stage of forest succession. Both yellow poplar and white pine are long-lived trees and may hold dominance here for a long time.

Virgin Forest

GSMNP contains the largest tracts of virgin forest in the eastern United States. About 20% of the Park's 500,000 acres exist in this pristine condition. Also called original forests and primary forests, virgin forests are climax forests that developed without man's interference and have existed undisturbed by him for many centuries. In truth, much of the virgin forest of GSMNP has experienced at least limited disturbance by man's activities. Bark stripping for tannin, single tree logging, limited grazing and set fires may have occurred. Nonetheless, virgin forest attributes still overwhelmingly dominate these relatively untouched forests.

Their value can not be overstated in terms of biodiversity, natural heritage and ecological understanding.

A large chunk of virgin forestland surrounds the main Tennessee-North Carolina divide from Charlies Bunion northeast to Mount Guyot covering the upper reaches of the Little Pigeon River above Greenbriar on the Tennessee side and the upper reaches of Bradley Fork and Raven Fork on the North Carolina side. This area together with the virgin forests surrounding Mt. LeConte comprises the largest chunk of virgin forest in the Park and in the eastern U. S.

The upper reaches of Cataloochee Creek and its branch, the Caldwell Fork support virgin forests, some of which were protected from loggers by the boogerman! Settler Robert Palmer (Palmer, Robert) lived a reclusive life on his remote farm in the hills above Caldwell Fork. Nicknamed Boogerman by his schoolmates, Palmer loved and protected his forestland, refusing all buy-out offers from lumber companies. As a result, some of the tallest and oldest trees in the East are found along the Boogerman Trail, named in his honor.

West of 441, most of the watershed of Deep Creek above its confluence with Pole Road Creek is virgin forest. This includes all the forest on the south side of Clingmans Dome Road, and though the north side of the dome was logged, its upper reaches still support virgin spruce-fir forests. Also on the north side of the main divide, the Road Prong valley supports virgin forest.

A couple of other virgin forest areas exist in the southwest part of the Park. They are on the upper north flanks of the main divide below Spence Field, and on the upper north face of the main divide below Mollies Ridge.

The virgin hemlock forest on the upper reaches of Cataloochee Cove is dominated by hemlock trees measuring 36, 40 and 46 inches in diameter. Applying our hemlock diameter/age equation of 10 x dbh suggests the ancient status of these trees, only a few of which have escaped the hemlock wooly adelgid. Here is a blackgum tree 34 inches in diameter. A 46-inch yellow poplar (roughly 200+ years old) halts our gaze. Rhododendron and mountain laurel, two acid-loving shrubs, comprise about 30% of the understory, along with some striped maple and witch hazel. Partridge berry and galax, also acid lovers, carpet portions of the forest floor.

Disturbed Old-Growth Forests

Disturbed old-growth forests (cross-hatch on the map)comprise about 8% of the Park's area. The largest, perhaps 30,000 acres, is located southwest of Cades Cove and includes the middle section of the Abrams Creek watershed, Rabbit Creek watershed and land flanking both sides of Parsons Branch Road. Portions of the southern slopes of Cove Mountain between Sugarlands Visitor Center and Metcalf Bottoms also support disturbed old-growth forest.

Here we find patches of old-growth trees surrounded by younger forests regenerating from former areas of dispersed settlement. The old-growth patches are fairly high in virgin forest attributes with huge, obviously ancient trees, but records show that burning, cattle grazing and logging occurred to some extent in many of theses areas.

The Rabbit Creek Trail traverses the disturbed old-growth forest southwest of Cades Cove. The trail follows an old road that once provided access to Cades Cove from the west. Don't try hiking this trail in winter, as there are several streams you must ford. Though ridges in this area reach only about 2300 feet elevation, the terrain is fairly rugged, not lending itself well to homesteading. Acid cove-hemlock forests grow along the streams. Oak-pine forests containing white pine, Virginia pine, white oak and chestnut oak often dominate exposed slopes and exposed ridgetops.

The Laurel Falls trail winds through the patch of disturbed old-growth forest between Sugarlands Visitor Center and Metcalf Bottoms. One of the most popular trails in the Park, it is paved for the first 1.3 miles. This first section passes through logged forest, on its way to 75-foot high Laurel Falls. Above this point, the trail loses its pavement and winds up into an old-growth classic cove hardwood forest with giant poplars, hemlocks, buckeyes and Fraser magnolias.

CHAPTER 7. SAMPLING THE FOREST

Much of the information in this book came from over 120 informal tree plots. The plots were established and measured without disturbing the forest--no markers, tags, flags or tracks. In this botanical Eden, besieged by ten million admiring visitors per year, protection of the environment is priority number one. The plots have become an enjoyable part of our hiking routine. It is something Jenny and I do together that provides time for a trail-side breather and the opportunity to re-acquaint ourselves with old tree friends. There is always something new.

But really, why measure the forest? First, it forces you to identify trees, a skill that will reward you for a lifetime. Second, it provides a written record of the site for later study so you can go back and determine successional stage and forest composition. Third, it functions as a journal, recording your visit, helping to create a memory. Finally, it could be a springboard toward a college degree or career in the field of natural resources. No, you are never too old! Here is one way to do it.

Foresters measure tree diameter (dbh) with a special diameter tape. You can buy one (year 2010) called the Jim-Gem Pocket Diameter Tape from Forestry Suppliers Inc. for about $12.00:

http://www.forestry-suppliers.com/search.asp?stext=diameter %20tape

You can also use your own body (it's always with you) as a measuring device like the Ancients did. Measure the distance between pinky finger and thumb of the outstretched hand (the ancient span, roughly 9 inches). Measure the distance from fingertips to elbow (the ancient cubit). Noah knew two spans equal one cubit. Measure the distance from wrist to finger tips. Compare these to a tree of known diameter. Remember tree diameter is measured at breast height (4.5 feet above the ground).

Hug a tree! Reach around a tree of known diameter to see where your two outstretched hands meet. Watch out for poison ivy vines! Large trees are hardest to measure. After estimating dbh of a big tree step back and use your eyes to confirm the estimate. With practice you will eventually be able to estimate dbh accurately enough just by looking at the tree. This is our ultimate goal, since it allows us to take a sample quickly and with minimal site disturbance. It is also a skill useful for winning free cold beverages when the hiking and measuring are done!

A circular tree plot one-tenth of an acre in area has a radius of 37 feet. Once again body parts come into play. Before hitting the woods measure out a line 37 feet long on a fairly flat, smooth surface like the front yard. Walk this line counting the number of steps (foresters and duelists call them paces) you take. Repeat the process several times until you know how many of your paces equal 37 feet. The average is about 15 paces for an adult.

While you're at it, lay out a 50 foot line and count your paces there too. Let's say 50 feet takes 20 of your paces. Now you know 10 paces equals 25 feet and 40 paces equals 100 feet, and so on. On steeply sloping terrain people tend to take smaller than normal steps. Correct your pace by double counting every tenth number when you pace up or down hill on steep slopes. For example count the tenth pace twice and the twentieth pace twice, etc. Double count every fifth pace for very steep slopes.

Back in the forest choose a plot center on the trail you are hiking. Pace out 37 feet from the plot center along the trail and begin identifying and measuring the canopy trees between you and the plot center. Your hiking partner can write down the information for you. Move around the circumference of the imaginary circle measuring trees between you and the plot center as you go.

Always be respectful of the environment, taking special care not to disturb the forest floor. If it looks like your measuring activities will disrupt the site, don't pace. Instead, estimate the plot radius visually. Scientific accuracy is not necessary to achieve our goals. Be sure to write down the location, elevation zone and landform of the plot center for future reference. By-the-way, many hand-held GPS units and some watches record accurate elevation on site.

Identifying trees is the most difficult part of recording a plot, but it is also the most rewarding. Knowing what trees to expect will help. Google topographic maps and the Forest Finder tell you what forest type you are likely to find. The description of that forest type will let you know what trees to expect. The disturbance map will help you decide what stage of forest succession you are likely to encounter.

A tree field guide and this book's tree descriptions provide great identification hints. Notice the shape of the leaf. Binoculars are handy for viewing high canopy foliage. Are the leaves simple or compound? Compound leaves look suspiciously uniform with leaflets arranged in two rows along a central leaf stem. Only a handful of southern Appalachian trees have compound leaves including ashes, hickories, walnuts, black locust and mountain ash. Are the leaves arranged in opposite pairs on the twig? Maples, ashes, dogwoods and buckeye are the most likely candidates in this category. The opposite arrangement is also displayed by the twigs, making winter identification easier. Look on the ground for autumn leaves cast off by surrounding trees. Distinctive bark patterns like the peeling golden bark of yellow birch, the smooth gray bark of beech and the ridge-and-furrow bark of hickory are easily recognized with practice.

Putting It All Together

Let's look at some examples of forests found in the Park to illustrate the idea of estimating forest successional stage and age from tree plots.

We establish a tenth-acre tree plot in a steep, protected waterless draw at about 2400 feet elevation. The Forest Finder indicates the mature forest here should be an acid cove-hemlock forest. This plot falls within the post-logging forest area of the Park, so its age may range between 70 and 110 years. This places it in the late pioneer or early intermediate stage of forest succession. There may be scattered older trees left standing by loggers. In the table below we list the canopy trees greater than 10 inches dbh.

68

Tree Species	Vertical Position	Shade Tolerance	Num. > 10" DBH	Ave. DBH (In.)	Est. Age (yrs.)
yellow poplar	dominant canopy	pioneer	9	19	75
black cherry	dispersed canopy	pioneer	1	10	60
red maple	dispersed canopy	intermediate	2	11	46
black birch	dispersed canopy	intermediate	2	10	-

A very distinctive leaf shape distinguishes yellow poplar, a pioneer tree, as the most numerous tree in the canopy with 9 individuals greater than 10 " dbh. This suggests a pioneer forest as does the fact that we have 10 pioneer trees, 4 intermediate trees and no large shade tolerant trees in the plot. Tree age information indicates the stand is probably less than 75 years old, an acceptable age for a forest in the late pioneer stage of succession. This is probably an early succession forest where the abundant yellow poplars will extend the length of the pioneer stage. There are numerous small hemlock trees in the subcanopy and understory of this plot (not listed in the table). We describe this forest as a low elevation acid cove-hemlock forest in the pioneer stage of forest succession.

As another example, here is a tree plot from a forest on an exposed slope at around 3400'.

Tree Species	Vertical Position	Shade Tolerance	Num. > 10" DBH	Ave. DBH (In.)	Est. Age (Yrs.)
black locust	dominant canopy	pioneer	2	17	77
red maple	dominant canopy	intermediate	2	13	48
white oak	dispersed canopy	intermediate	2	10	
chestnut oak	dispersed canopy	intermediate	1	26	
blackgum	dispersed canopy	intermediate	1	10	

This plot contains 2 pioneer trees, 6 intermediate trees and no shade tolerant trees. The mix suggests a stand in the intermediate stage of forest succession between 100 and 200 years old. Tree age data suggest the black locust (compound leaves composing a thin, battered-looking crown) is close to a century old, the red maples (opposite leaves) are younger and the chestnut oak (distinctive leaf shape and deeply ridged bark) at 26 inches is probably over a century old. Exposed slopes are the former habitat of the American chestnut tree. The chestnut trees were wiped out by chestnut blight around 50 years ago. The red maples and the blackgum may be replacement trees growing into the gaps left by the chestnuts. The big chestnut oak is likely a remnant of the former mature chestnut oak-hickory-red maple forest indicated by the Forest Finder as the mature forest for this elevation and topographic position. We describe this forest as a <u>middle elevation chestnut oak-hickory-red maple forest in the intermediate stage of forest succession</u>.

As a final example, we have a stream-side forest at 4200 feet elevation on the North Carolina side of the main divide. In this example we have divided yellow buckeye and sugar maple each into two diameter groups since their diameter ranges seem to indicate two different age groups.

Tree Species	Vertical Position	Shade Tolerance	Num. > 10" DBH	Ave. DBH (In.)	Est. Age (yrs.)
yellow birch	dominant canopy	intermediate	3	13	
yellow buckeye	dominant canopy	tolerant	2	16.5	
yellow buckeye	dominant canopy	tolerant	2	32	
sugar maple	dominant canopy	tolerant	2	10	
sugar maple	dominant canopy	tolerant	1	36	
Eastern hemlock	dispersed canopy	tolerant	3	12	
basswood	dispersed canopy	tolerant	1	23	

The Forest Finder tells us this is the realm of the cool cove forest, and the species mix from the plot supports this. The large number of shade tolerant trees suggests at least a mature forest (200-250 years old). This site is designated as post-settlement forest on our forest disturbance map, so we hesitate to class it as a virgin climax forest. We describe it as a <u>middle elevation cool cove forest in the mature stage of forest succession.</u>

After recording a forest tree plot, come back to camp. Brew a hot cup of coffee and put your feet up or in a mountain stream. While your companion strums the dulcimer, list the trees from the plot in a table similar to those in the examples. The forest composition information in the table will indicate the approximate stage of forest succession of the stand. Use the Google topo map you printed out to find the site's elevation. Refer to the Forest Finder to determine the mature forest you are likely to find on the site. The disturbance map will give clues to the type and approximate age of the forest from which your sample plot is derived. Finally, apply the tree age equations to pioneer trees in the plot. Now describe the forest in terms of type and successional stage. Excellent work!

CHAPTER 8. EXOTIC TREE PESTS

Man's activities have brought about profound changes in the forests of GSMNP. In the chapter on forest age we looked at effects of land clearing and logging on age and composition of the Park's forests. We will now look at the impact of exotic tree diseases, the fourth important influence on the forests of GSMNP.

Beginning around the turn of the 20th century, a series of devastating exotic tree diseases accidentally entered North America. These diseases existed in ecological balance in their native lands where host trees they attacked had enough resistance to ensure recovery. North American forests provided tree species suitable as hosts to the diseases, but with little or no inbred resistance to their onslaught. Consequently, the exotic diseases virtually wiped out their North American host species creating irrevocable rents in the forest. We will consider the four most important of these forest scourges in the sequence they occurred, and discuss changes they brought about.

Chestnut Blight

Considered by many the most important hardwood tree in North America, the American chestnut tree was a very fast grower, outstripping even yellow poplar in full sunlight. Intermediate in shade tolerance, it had the ability to persist in the subcanopy until an opening occurred, filling the opening ahead of all other trees. Its deep taproot enhanced its survival on both moist and dry sites. These characteristics and its vigorous sprouting ability gave American chestnut dominance in several southern Appalachian forest environments.

In the low elevation zone (1500-2500'), American chestnut was a dispersed canopy tree in forests on creek flats, in draws and on protected slopes and protected ridgetops. It dominated forests on exposed slopes and exposed ridgetops in both low and middle elevation zones. These exposed slope and ridgetop forests were called chestnut oak-chestnut forests, northern red oak-chestnut forests and white oak-chestnut forests by Whittaker. In forests where it occurred, chestnut comprised 30 to 60 percent of the canopy trees.

Like yellow poplar and white pine, American chestnut was long lived, persisting into the climax forest. Giants exceeding 10 feet in diameter graced the canopies of virgin mountain forests, producing annually an incredibly abundant crop of nutritious chestnuts. Mountain folk depended on chestnuts for food for themselves and their animals. Income from the sale of chestnuts and the tannin-rich tree bark provided cash for necessities they could not grow or make. Bear, deer, turkey, squirrel and other wild animals fattened on the chestnut crop, and their populations reflected the rich abundance of this food source.

Around 1904, Asian chestnut trees imported from China or Japan accidentally introduced the chestnut blight into North America. Caused by the fungus *Cryphonectria parasitica (*formerly *Endothia parasitica)*, the blight creates trunk sores called cankers that destroy the tree's life-giving cambium layer just under the bark. American chestnut trees had no resistance against this foreign invader, which wiped out virtually every American chestnut tree in eastern North America by 1950. Unaffected by the blight, the root systems of chestnut trees still cling to life sending up sprouts from battered stumps where they persist in the understory until the blight finds them again.

Removal of the chestnut crop made the hard life of the mountain farmer harder, and it has been said the rise of moonshining was to some extent the mountaineer's effort to recoup income deprived him by the blight. Populations of wildlife that depended on the chestnut crop plummeted, never to fully recover. In summary, loss of the American chestnut tree has been the most devastating tree disaster in America's history...so far.

As chestnut trees succumbed, they left gaping openings in the forest canopy now being filled by trees that were major associates of the chestnut. On moist sites like creek flats, draws and protected slopes, northern red oak, red maple and hemlock are the major replacement trees. On dryer sites like exposed slopes and ridgetops, oaks, especially chestnut oak and red maple have filled this role.

Forest Finder forest types reflect the changes in composition that have occurred on former chestnut sites. The chestnut oak-hickory-red maple forest and northern red oak-hickory-red maple forest found on exposed slopes in the low and middle elevation zones cover much of the area American chestnut once dominated. As these forests mature, the oaks will remain as dominant canopy trees in the climax forest, while red maple will eventually shift from dominant canopy to dispersed canopy as it is eventually replaced by more shade tolerant trees like the hickories.

When you hike trails on exposed slopes and ridgetops in the Smokies, look for chestnut tree sprouts in the forest understory as indicators of the former chestnut forest. The wrist-size sprouts usually occur in clumps emanating from a challenged root system. Sometimes the sprouts actually produce flowers and fruit, but the blight eventually attacks, surrounding sections of the trunk with orange colored cankers. Close examination reveals tiny orange spots, each a fruiting body of the fungus whose network of root-like mycelia eventually encircles the trunk and kills the sprout.

Initial efforts to beat the chestnut blight began in the 1920's when the U. S. Department of Agriculture crossed Chinese and Japanese chestnut trees with American trees, but few of these crosses proved blight-resistant. In the late 1970's French scientists discovered a virus that attacked the blight fungus giving protection to inoculated American chestnut trees. Attempts to get this "hypovirus" to spread to American trees failed, though work on the project continues today.

Since the early 1990's genetic engineers have focused on finding genes from other plants capable of fighting back against the chestnut blight fungus. The genes would be inserted into American chestnut tree cells which would be cloned in the laboratory and grown into blight-resistant trees. This potentially promising approach has been hampered by the stubbornness of the American chestnut tree itself. Unlike some of its fellow trees, the American chestnut has proven very difficult to clone, something researchers did not expect. Ultimately genetic engineering may provide the best solution to the problem, but it is not likely to occur soon.

The current best hope for the American chestnut tree began in the late 1970's when Dr. Charles Burnham (Burnham, Dr. Charles) founder of the American Chestnut Foundation proposed a previously proven plant breeding technique called backcrossing for saving the tree. The objective of backcrossing is to get the blight-resistant genes carried by the Chinese chestnut tree into the American chestnut tree by cross breeding the two trees, followed by generations of backcrossing to the American parent. According to Dr. Burnham, if done correctly, backcrossing should result in an American chestnut tree that incorporates the blight resistance of Chinese chestnuts and the outstanding tree form of the American tree.

Accordingly, American Chestnut Foundation researchers began combing the countryside for surviving American chestnut trees for incorporation into the backcrossing program. They eventually located about 500 trees, hopefully enough to ensure genetic diversity in the future population of blight-resistant chestnuts. These trees were first crossed with Chinese chestnut trees producing a generation of hybrids. The hybrids were grown for about 6 years and then inoculated with the blight to test for resistance. Survivors were then backcrossed with American chestnut trees and another round of testing occurred. This backcrossing and testing cycle happened a total of 3 times resulting in a tree that was about fifteen sixteenths American chestnut and showed fairly good blight resistance. These trees were then crossed with each other and tested two times resulting in the final product, a blight-resistant tree that is fifteen sixteenths American.

Though it takes about 6 years for each round of backcrossing and testing, Foundation breeders have been working on the project for some time and actually planted the first group of blight-resistant seedlings in 2008. It appears patience and persistence is paying off. The tortoise may win the race again, and with luck, we may eat American chestnuts gathered from the forest before another human generation has passed!

Balsam Wooly Adelgid

The high country of GSMNP begins at 4500 feet elevation, extending up to the 6643 foot summit of Clingmans Dome. This is the realm of the spruce-fir and Fraser fir forests that covered extensive areas of eastern North America during the last ice age. As glaciers retreated, the warming climate chased the spruce-fir forest up into islands of cooler high country, isolating it from similar forests to the north. As a result several unique plants and animals developed here. Fraser fir is one of these unique to the southern Appalachians, differing from the more common balsam fir found further north.

The park contains 75% of all natural Fraser fir forests in existence. This tree dominated the forests above 6000 feet elevation. Between 5000 and 6000 feet it was co-dominant with red spruce in forests that also include yellow birch, pin cherry and mountain ash.

In 1963 the Park Service noticed Fraser firs on Mount Sterling were being attacked by the balsam wooly adelgid (*Adelges piceae*), an insect native to central Europe and accidentally introduced into this country around 1900. Since then, all Fraser fir forests have been infested by this pest, resulting in the death of 90% of the mature Fraser firs in most Park locations.

A drive through the high country today reveals hundreds of graying dead Fraser fir trunks glistening on mountain flanks. Loss of the firs has allowed strong winds to damage many of the red spruce trees once protected by their wind-hardy associates. In some stands, fir seedlings and saplings are numerous, filling openings created by dead trees. Young firs are immune to attack until they develop bark fissures at maturity (about 20 years). Then they succumb to the adelgid as part of a recurring boom and bust cycle resulting in the gradual elimination of fir. On other sites, hobblebush and thornless blackberry have proliferated in the absence of the fir canopy. How these forests will ultimately adapt to loss of the Fraser fir is presently unknown.

An aphid-like insect, the balsam wooly adelgid inserts its sucking apparatus into cracks in the bark and sucks sap from the tree. It injects salivary compounds causing an allergic reaction that severely disrupts the tree's ability to move water through its sapwood. Infestation usually kills the tree in two to seven years.

There are only females in the bizarre world of the wooly adelgid, a strategy tailor-made for efficiency in reproduction. The insects are tiny (.03 inches long) and covered with waxy white threads that look like a wooly mass. Each female can lay 100 or more eggs up to three times a year.

Fraser firs have no natural defense mechanisms against this voracious killer, and Park officials have been frustrated by the lack of practical control methods. A mild detergent spray readily kills the adelgid by dissolving its waxy wool coat, but it is impossible to spray thousands of acres of fir trees on a regular basis. Insecticides also kill the adelgid and commercial growers of Fraser fir Christmas trees use these chemicals with success, but they are neither economically practical nor environmentally suitable for widespread use in the Park.

The Park has established a genetic plantation for Fraser fir where pesticides are used to maintain the trees. The plantation will help preserve the tree's unique genetic character so it can be re-introduced when effective control measures are developed.

Beech Bark Disease

American beech grows at nearly all elevations in the Park, but dominates only the beech gap forest type of the high elevation zone. Here it forms a stunted canopy along with lesser amounts of mountain silverbell, yellow birch and occasionally yellow buckeye. The subcanopy and understory are usually sparse allowing a rich growth of sedges, ferns and wildflowers to flourish on the ground below.

American beech is also a canopy tree in the northern hardwood forest found in ravines and on north slopes in the high elevation zone. In these forests it co-dominates with yellow birch, yellow buckeye and occasionally red spruce.

In the late 1980's, diseased beech trees were observed in the Park, but the cause remained undiscovered until 1993 when it was determined that the European beech bark scale insect *Cryptococcus fagisuga* and a *Nectria* fungus were responsible for the deaths of the beech trees. The scale insects make tiny punctures in the bark and begin sucking sap from the tree. This stresses the tree, but usually doesn't kill it. The punctures provide entry points for the Nectria fungus which attacks and eventually does kill the tree within 1- 4 years of initial attack.

The disease progresses in two stages. The <u>killing front stage</u> occurs with initial exposure to the disease. Most of the beech tops are killed back, and their roots respond with prolific sprouting creating a dense young beech forest. Eventually the disease returns to attack the sprout forest in the <u>aftermath stage</u> where it once again decimates the beeches, often killing the entire tree, roots and all.

Not all beech trees succumb to beech bark disease. USDA scientists have determined that some trees have natural resistance and this resistance can be passed down to progeny. Efforts to breed resistant beech trees are now underway and provide what is currently considered the best hope for defeat of beech bark disease.

Hemlock Wooly Adelgid

Eastern hemlock is often found near water. In the southern Appalachians it is a dispersed canopy tree in low elevation river cove forests. It dominates the canopy on low elevation creek flats and middle elevation protected slopes in the acid cove-hemlock forest. The Park supports about 90,000 acres of forests containing significant numbers of hemlocks. There are over 3000 acres of virgin hemlock forest here.

Hemlock is undesirable for lumber because it splits readily; nonetheless, loggers cut a lot of this tree for paper pulp. Old giants too large for pulping were often left, resulting in some very large and probably very old specimens in the Park. The tannin-rich bark of hemlock was once in high demand by the leather tanning industry.

Hemlock's affinity for streams provides benefits to animals that live there. Streams in hemlock forests support more kinds of aquatic invertebrates than those in hardwood forests. The native brook trout is three times more abundant here than in hardwood forest streams, a result of the cooler, oxygen-rich water found below the deep shade of hemlocks. Many birds prefer hemlock streamside forests for nesting, and the black-throated green warbler depends on hemlocks exclusively for both feeding and nesting sites as does the ruffed grouse.

The hemlock wooly adelgid (*Adelges tsugae*), an aphid-like insect native to Japan and China, was first spotted on hemlock trees in British Columbia, Canada, in the 1920's, but it did little damage to the western hemlock trees there. The Park Service discovered it on Eastern hemlocks near Fontana dam in 2002. Since then the hemlock wooly adelgid (HWA) has spread throughout GSMNP.

Similar to its relative the balsam wooly adelgid, the HWA also covers itself with waxy white hairs. It attaches to the base of a hemlock needle and sucks sap from the tree. Infested trees usually die in three to five years.

Many of the old giants spared by loggers have already fallen to HWA. A hike up Anthony Creek Trail reveals 40-inch hemlocks towering above the forest floor with crowns devoid of needles, waiting for decay and wind to bring them crashing earthward. The Cataloochee district supports some of the largest Eastern hemlocks in the world, but even now the HWA is working its way through these stands, decimating the magnificent monarchs. Loss of these giants is forever.

Currently the Park Service uses a multi-prong attack plan against HWA. In areas accessible by roads, trees are sprayed with a soap solution that dissolves the bug's waxy coating and kills it. The entire tree crown must be sprayed and the treatment lasts only about six months. In more remote areas, chemicals are injected into the soil at the tree base. The tree pulls the chemicals up into its needles where the HWA ingests them and dies. This treatment is done by hand, costs about $75.00 per tree and lasts about one year.

Two kinds of predatory beetles are being used to fight HWA. *Laricobius nigrinus,* nicknamed "Larry" by the Park Service, is native to the Northwestern U.S. where it effectively preys on adelgids there. *Sasajiscymnus tsugae* nicknamed "ST" is an Asia native that specifically preys on HWA in its native land. Both of these biocontrol beetles are raised at the University of Tennessee and then released into the Park. So far, over 350,000 beetles have been released, but the process is slow requiring 5 to10 years for the biocontrol beetles to become permanently established.

The Park Service reports good results against HWA in areas where chemical injection and biocontrol beetles are used together. Moist weather is also significant in helping the hemlocks fight off HWA attacks. The Park Service is to be commended for its aggressive and timely stand against this plague of Biblical proportions.

Arnold Arboretum reports Chinese hemlock (*Tsuga chinensis*) shows excellent resistance to HWA. Can Chinese hemlock step in to replace native hemlocks? This is a strange prospect, like fighting fire with fire, but in a shrinking world where all things, especially pests, are shared, such a solution might prove to be our only alternative. Time will tell.

Hemlock forests grow on low elevation creek flats and on middle elevation protected slopes. Hemlock is the dominant tree in these forests. The most common associates of hemlock are white pine, red maple, black birch, white oak and yellow poplar. As the hemlocks die off they will likely be replaced by their shade-intermediate associates like white pine, red maple, black birch and white oak. Of these, white pine, yellow poplar and white oak are likely to remain in the canopy after a century of growth. Conversion of hemlock forests to hardwood forests will result in loss of the unique characteristics that made life possible for animals dependent on hemlocks. One loss begets another.

The exotic pests discussed in this chapter are significant because they eliminate major forest components. Whole forest types are disappearing as a result; along with the animals that depend on these environments for survival. For example, the high elevation zone of the park (4500'-6500+') once supported about 5 different major forest types. With the advent of balsam wooly adelgid and beech bark disease, only 3 forest types remain intact. Hemlock wooly adelgid will remove an entire forest type (hemlock forest) and reduce tree diversity in at least 4 more forest types. The loss of species extends through the food chain, and we probably won't know its full extent for some time

We must devise a method to determine which native tree will be attacked next. This means looking for similarities in the patterns of origin, import and spread of these exotic killers. We must become familiar with the flora and fauna of places most likely to harbor the next pest. We must somehow learn to anticipate and deactivate the next pest on the horizon. Hypovirulent fungus strains and biocontrol predators might be the answer. Perhaps someday we can use genetic engineering to create super predators to nip exotic pests in the bud before they decimate our forests. In the mean time we must brace for the changes that will inevitably come.

CHAPTER 9. FOREST DESCRIPTIONS

As you read about the following forest types, please refer to Appendix 2, Master List of Plants, to verify tree and shrub name abbreviations used in the forest tables.

Also note that the forest examples listed for each forest type don't always match exactly with the initial forest description. Each example represents an actual forest plot taken on site in the Park. The plots verify that nature always provides us with exceptions to our "rules" that attempt to define her parameters; a fact that is sometimes frustrating, but always refreshing!

PAGES

River Cove Forest

Forest Types Included from the Great Smoky Mountains National Park All Taxa Biodiversity Inventory (http://www.dlia.org/index.shtml):

App. Montane Alluvial Forest
App. Montane Alluvial Forest (Oconaluftee, Cades Cove)
Montane Sweetgum Alluvial Forest

ELE	DOM. CANOPY TREES	DISP. CANOPY TREES	SUB-CANOPY TREES	UNDER-STORY TREES & SHRUBS
1500-2500 '	Sycamore Y. Poplar Red Maple B. Birch Hemlock	<u>Lowest Elevations</u> Green Ash River Birch Sweetgum B. Cherry B. Walnut Shingle Oak <u>Rich River Coves</u> B. Cherry Sug. Maple White Ash Basswood Buckeye Cuc-tree Y. Birch N. Red Oak Bitt. Hick. Beech Silverbell <u>Dry Acidic Coves</u> W. Oak Scar. Oak W. Pine Va. Pine	Sourwood Boxelder	Hornbeam R. Rhodo. F. Dogwood Witch Hazel Dog Hobble

Forest Summary

- Found along rivers in the low elevation zone.
- American sycamore is almost always in the canopy.
- American hornbeam is almost always in the understory.
- Rosebay rhododendron is often prominent in the understory.

Forest Description

River cove forests grow in the low elevation zone (1500-2500') on bottoms along the Park's river-size streams (Oconaluftee River, Little River, West Prong Little Pigeon River, Little Pigeon River, Cataloochee Creek and lower Abrams Creek), and along low elevation prongs like Middle Prong of Little River, Big Creek and Bradley Fork. For the most part, river cove forests occupy the Park's boundary. This is not surprising since the towering Unaka Range of the southern Appalachian Mountains forms the high central backbone of the Park, relegating the low elevation zone to the Park's outer perimeter. All of the Park's visitor centers and developed campgrounds except Balsam campground are in the low elevation zone along streams that support river cove forest.

There are no virgin river cove forests in the Park. River bottoms, lower prong coves and creek flats were the first places cleared for homes, fields and pastures when settlers arrived here in the early 1800's. In the early 1900's large scale logging operations clearcut thousands of acres of the remaining forests. However, there are places along all the Park's rivers where large old trees can be found hugging the river bank, like the big sycamores (80 inches in diameter), cucumbertrees (30 inches) and basswoods (38 inches) along the Oconaluftee River near the Oconaluftee Village and Visitor Center. These huge trees predate both the corporate logging era (1900-1939) and the Park's establishment (1934).

Today most river cove forests appear to be in the late pioneer or early intermediate stage of forest succession (about 80-120 years old). Trees with intermediate shade tolerance ratings like sycamore, red maple, white pine, oaks and black birch have attained canopy dominance and frequently outnumber the pioneer trees like poplar, cucumbertree, sweetgum and black cherry. Many yellow poplars in these low elevation river cove forests average around 19 inches in diameter with an approximate age of 75 years (age $=5$ X dbh-20 years) that roughly coincides with the Park's establishment or slightly before when most of the logging ceased. As previously mentioned, you are likely to find a few older larger trees here and there in these forests. Thirty-inch diameter shade tolerant trees like hemlock or buckeye growing among much smaller pioneer and intermediate trees are obviously out of successional sequence. They were overlooked by both settlers and loggers. What stories could they tell?

American sycamore is nearly always a canopy tree in river cove forests and is diagnostic of this forest type. Its stark white upper trunk visibly proclaims its presence. American hornbeam, also known as muscle-wood for its muscular gray trunk, is another tree indicative of the river cove forest, where it makes its permanent home in the understory. Both trees are also characteristic of lowland river forests in the Piedmont Province to the south and east, and both drop out of the cove forest mix around 2500 feet elevation.

Other trees abundant in less mountainous areas outside the Park may be found here. Though not as diagnostic as sycamore and hornbeam, sweetgum, river birch, black walnut and boxelder may be present. Like sycamore and hornbeam they will drop out before the 2500 foot elevation level is reached.

Red maple, the most widely distributed tree in the eastern United States, is usually well represented in the canopy of the river cove forest. Also from the lowlands, it will remain abundant in coves and along creeks up into higher elevations occupying all but the highest and driest places in the Park.

Black walnut in these river bottoms gives living testimony to man's presence. Edible black walnuts were prized by Cherokee Indians and settlers. The great American botanist William Bartram, roaming primitive America during the late 1700's, noted abundant black walnut trees in river bottoms on former Indian town sites.

The wood of black walnut is prized for its workability and dark beauty. Undoubtedly man has had a hand in the spread of this beautiful and valuable bottomland tree.

On rich river bottom sites where moisture and nutrients are abundant, trees of the classic cove hardwood forest found higher up the cove join sycamore and hornbeam. Basswood, hemlock, mountain silverbell, sugar maple and white ash often add to the diversity of species.

Conversely, on dryer, less fertile and more acidic sites, especially along prong-size streams with less bottomland; white pine, Virginia pine and the oaks can be more abundant in the low elevation river cove canopy. White pine and the oaks are intermediate in shade tolerance and long lived, persisting where they occur into the mature forest stage of succession and beyond. Sourwood, an acid-loving species often appears in the subcanopy on these sites, and rhododendron may dominate the understory.

Shingle oak (*Quercus imbricaria*) is found in low elevation river cove forests in just two locations in the Park; along Abrams creek in Cades Cove and along the Oconaluftee River near the Oconaluftee Visitor Center. Its occurrence constitutes a unique and rare category of low elevation river cove forest that may be the only example of this forest type in the world. Here shingle oak shares the canopy with sycamore, box elder, red maple and yellow poplar with a sparse understory of mostly canopy tree seedlings. It is believed that cattle grazing has influenced the composition of this forest.

Examples of River Cove Forests

Middle Prong

This site is located along the Middle Prong (near Tremont) of Little River (a prong-size stream) about a half mile north of the Middle Prong parking lot where the hiking trail begins. The largest poplars average 30 inches in diameter, giving a rough age estimate of about 150 years (5 X dbh). Both the white ash (26") and the bitternut hickory (16") also appear old. The remaining trees are relatively small suggesting a forest of two ages. Middle Prong was logged between 1926 and 1939.

ELE	DOM. CANOPY	DISP. CANOPY	SUB-CANOPY	UNDER-STORY TREES & SHRUBS
1700'	Y. Poplar W. Ash Silverbell	Bitt. Hick. Sycamore Sweetgum Y. Birch	Red Maple Hemlock	Hornbeam F. Dogwood Spicebush

Oconaluftee River

From the Oconaluftee Visitor Center to just north of Collins Creek, the Oconaluftee River traverses the low elevation zone. At Oconaluftee Visitor Center (1800'), once the site of a Cherokee Indian village, the river is flanked by wide fertile bottomland. The forest adjacent to the river and Visitor Center appears relatively old with some large-diameter sycamore and basswood trees. Trees more common in the classic cove hardwood forest like bitternut hickory, sugar maple and basswood accompany the sycamore and hornbeam on this rich site as well as yellow birch from higher up. This river rises directly to the peak of the Smokies where high-elevation tree seeds may be washed or blown down the river to germinate in the low-elevation zone.

ELE	DOM. CANOPY TREES	DISP. CANOPY TREES	SUB-CANOPY	UNDER-STORY TREES & SHRUBS
2000'	Sycamore Y. Poplar Basswood	W. Oak Bitt. Hick. Hemlock Sug. Maple Beech B. Cherry Cuc-tree Red Maple Y. Birch	Boxelder Persimmon Fraser Mag.	Hornbeam F. Dogwood R. Rhodo. Doghobble Mt. Holly

Elkmont Campground

Elkmont campground is located on the Little River at its junction with Jakes Creek. At the campground, the river is actually prong-size. The biggest poplar here is 28" diameter giving a rough age estimate of 140 years. Here is a 30-inch white pine and there a 16-inch hemlock, both fairly old trees. Younger trees surround these old ones on this site which was once the scene of a bustling logging town and later the playground of prosperous lumber company executives. The part of the forest sampled has more white pine, scarlet oak and northern red oak, than the other forest examples, suggesting a slightly drier, less fertile, possibly more acidic environment. The presence of sourwood, an acid-loving subcanopy tree found on dry sites, reinforces this notion, as does the presence of pitch pine.

ELE	DOM. CANOPY TREES	DISP. CANOPY TREES	SUB-CANOPY	UNDER-STORY TREES & SHRUBS
2250 '	Y. Poplar Red Maple N. Red Oak	Sycamore W. Pine Scar. Oak Hemlock B. Birch Pitch Pine	Sourwood	Hornbeam F. Dogwood

Acid Cove-Hemlock Forest

Forest Types Included from the Great Smoky Mountains National Park All Taxa Biodiversity Inventory (http://www.dlia.org/index.shtml):

Southern Appalachian Acid Cove Forest (Typic Type)
Southern Appalachian Acid Cove Forest (Silverbell Type)
Southern Appalachian Eastern Hemlock Forest (Typic Type)
Southern Appalachian Eastern Hemlock Forest (W. Pine Type)
Southern Appalachian Acidic Mixed Hardwood Forest

ELE.	DOM. CANOPY TREES	DISP. CANOPY TREES	SUB-CANOPY TREES	UNDER-STORY TREES & SHRUBS
1500'-2500'	Hemlock Y. Poplar B. Birch Red Maple	Moist Sites Basswood Buckeye W. Ash Beech Dryer Sites W. Pine W. Oak N. Red Oak Blackgum	Fraser Mag. Sourwood A. Holly	R. Rhodo. Mt. Laurel Doghobble F. Dogwood
2500-4500'	Hemlock Silverbell Sug.Maple	Beech Y. Birch Red Maple B.Cherry Buckeye	Fraser Mag.	R. Rhodo. Str. Maple

Forest Summary

- Found on <u>acidic</u> sites.
- Found on creek flats and protected (often steep) slopes in the low and middle elevation zones.

- Hemlock dominates the canopy along with three or fewer associates.
- Acid-loving species like Heath family members common.
- Rosebay rhododendron frequently dominates the understory.
- At successional maturity, hemlock dominates exclusively.
- The hemlock wooly adelgid is presently decimating this forest type.

Detailed Description

Acid cove forests are distinguished from hemlock forests in the All Taxa Biodiversity Inventory that describes the Park's forests in detail. <u>Acid cove forests</u> are abundant in the Park, occurring along many streams as they tumble down the mountain through rocks like those of the Anakeesta Formation where acidic compounds leach into the surrounding soil. <u>Hemlock forests</u> also grow on moist acidic sites, but hemlock dominates the canopy exclusively, refusing to share with the hardwoods.

In reality, the difference between these two forest types may be a matter of successional stage, with acid cove forests representing the intermediate stage of forest succession in what will eventually become a mature hemlock forest. Most of the Park's designated hemlock forests are very old forests (either virgin forests or disturbed old-growth forests) located on the same kinds of sites that acid cove forests occupy in more recently disturbed (younger) sections of the Park.

Cataloochee provides a good example. Its middle elevation streams support the largest chunk of hemlock forest in the Park. These are virgin forests, and they grow on sites where acid cove forests occur elsewhere. This book combines the two forest types into one; the <u>acid cove-hemlock forest</u> to indicate their successional relationship, and to anticipate the reduced presence of hemlock in the future.

In the low elevation zone (1500-2500'), acid cove-hemlock forests grow on acidic sites along streams, especially creek flats. In the middle elevation zone they are found on creek flats and protected slopes, especially <u>steep</u> protected slopes. During early stages of succession, hemlock shares the dominant canopy with poplar, black birch and red maple on more moist sites, and with white pine and oaks on dryer sites. American sycamore and American hornbeam, trees diagnostic of the river cove forest are usually <u>absent</u> from the acid cove-hemlock forest.

The subcanopy of acid cove-hemlock forests is usually dominated by acid-loving plants like sourwood and American holly. Rhododendron is almost always present in the understory, and often dominant there. Mountain laurel and doghobble characteristically share the understory with rhododendron as well as its acid-loving tendency. Unlike classic cove hardwood forests, acid cove-hemlock forests usually lack a rich herbaceous layer.

As the acid cove-hemlock forest matures, hemlock assumes exclusive canopy dominance simply by virtue of its great size and age. It just outlasts everything else. At this late stage of succession, its dispersed canopy cohorts are likely to be other shade tolerant trees like buckeye, basswood and beech along with just a few huge poplars and white pines, both long-lived trees from earlier successional stages.

It is not uncommon to find examples of both river cove forest and acid cove-hemlock forest growing in the low elevation zone along the same stream as conditions of soil acidity vary with location. In fact, nature regularly refuses to be pinned down to a strict regimen of classification, changing along with the environmental conditions that sustain her. But she does exhibit elevational continuity.

As we follow a mountain river upstream we expect first to encounter river cove forest where sycamore and hornbeam are characteristic along with a variety of lowland and mountain trees.

With increasing elevation, the river becomes a prong loosing much of its bottomland, becoming narrower, steeper and more musical. We walk through acid pockets lacking sycamore and hornbeam where hemlock is prominent in the canopy with much rhododendron and mountain laurel below.

As we ascend into the middle elevation zone at around 2500', the dominant canopy trees of the acid cove-hemlock forest change. Yellow poplar and white pine drop out. Mountain silverbell becomes more common along with sugar maple in places. The acid-loving rhododendron remains as a prominent understory component.

On less acidic stream sites, the classic cove hardwood forest appears above 2500 feet elevation. Basswood, white ash and sugar maple become more abundant along with yellow poplar and some hemlock. Still higher up, we realize yellow poplar, cucumber tree and others have dropped out of the classic cove hardwood mix. Basswood remains and buckeye and yellow birch are now more abundant as we transition to the cool cove forest, especially on the south-facing North Carolina side of the main divide. By now our prong is a creek and is growing smaller. Above around 4500' elevation the creek may become a waterless ravine. Only a few hardwood trees remain. Yellow birch, yellow buckeye and American beech dominate, often with red spruce, especially on the north-facing Tennessee side of the main divide. We have entered the northern hardwood forest.

Yellow poplar is the prominent pioneer tree in low elevation acid cove-hemlock forests on moist acidic sites. It would dominate the site during the pioneer stage of forest succession (50-100 years) as forest succession advanced on abandoned fields or cut-over land. At age 80 years (time elapsed since the Park's establishment) we would expect dominant canopy poplars to be in the 19-20 inch diameter range. We would look for intermediates like red maple, blackgum and black birch in the dispersed canopy and subcanopy ready to steal dominance from the poplars in a few years. Hemlocks, the future inheritors of the site would fill the subcanopy. By the mature stage of succession (200-250 years) they will dominate the canopy as the forest approaches climax.

Eastern hemlock is disappearing from southern Appalachian forests along with other beautiful, valuable, seemingly indispensable tree species. The potential for more species devastation is firmly on the horizon as the world continues to share pathogens at an alarming rate. Mass extinctions have been common in earth's history, from the trilobite die-offs of the late Cambrian Period to the more recent disappearance of Pleistocene mega-fauna. It is hoped that there will be people around in the future to read about this potential latest episode!

Examples of Acid Cove-Hemlock Forest

Anthony Creek

Take the Anthony Creek Trail through the picnic area and beyond. This example of a dryer acid cove-hemlock forest is located on the flat formed by Anthony Creek. Near the picnic area, white oak, chestnut oak and big white pines accompany hemlock in the canopy. As we ascend the trail to around 2300 feet, 30-inch hemlocks completely dominate, but they give silent testimony to the work of the hemlock wooly adelgid.

ELE.	DOM. CANOPY TREES	DISPERSED CANOPY TREES	SUB-CANOPY TREES	UNDER-STORY TREES & SHRUBS
2000'	Hemlock W. Oak Chest. Oak	W. Pine Red Maple	Sourwood	Dogwood R. Rhodo.

Rough Fork

Jenny and I hike along the Rough Fork just upstream from its junction with Cataloochee Creek. We establish a snack and a plot at about 2800 feet elevation. Disaster has struck because I am out of Debbie cakes. Forced to subsist on healthful trail mix from Jenny's pack, I resolve to face hardship with stoic determination as did the pioneers before me!

This is a virgin acid cove-hemlock forest. The hemlocks average over 30 inches in diameter with one whopper reaching 46 inches. Our diameter/age equation for hemlock (diameter times 10) probably overstates the giant's age a bit at 460 years, though there are hemlocks older than this in GSMNP. Hemlock dominates here by virtue of its great size and age, but the point is mute as we stand gaping at the dead crowns of these giant trees. They are draped with long lichen filaments instead of hemlock needles. There are a couple of big buckeyes here, 24 and 32 inches respectively.

The presence of hornbeam in the understory is another curiosity. Hornbeam is usually found lower down on larger, less acidic streams, but mother nature knows what she is doing, so we accept her defiance of our tidy system of classification.

ELE.	DOM. CANOPY TREES	DISP. CANOPY TREES	SUB-CANOPY TREES	UNDER-STORY TREES & SHRUBS
2800'	Hemlock	Y. Birch Silverbell Buckeye	Red Maple	R. Rhodo. Doghobble Hornbeam

Kephart Prong

The Kephart Prong Trail departs from Highway 441 at around 2700 feet elevation. The trail follows Kephart Prong, named for Horace Kephart, author of <u>Our Southern Highlanders</u>, a book chronicling the lives of mountain people and the changes ushered in by the corporate logging boom that opened the mountains up to the outside world.

About 1.5 miles up the trail, the surrounding forest appears less disturbed by man than down below. There are some big trees in this plot. A couple of 20-inch hemlocks (adelgid victims) appear to be well over a century old. They share the dominant canopy with black birch and yellow birch, several of which are in the 25-inch diameter range. Here is a 27-inch yellow poplar, there a 20-

inch black cherry. Rhododendron covers about 70% of the understory, a characteristic of the acid cove-hemlock forest.

ELE.	DOM. CANOPY TREES	DISP. CANOPY TREES	SUB-CANOPY TREES	UNDER-STORY TREES & SHRUBS
3300'	Hemlock B. Birch Y. Birch	Y. Poplar Red Maple Basswood B. Cherry	Young canopy trees	R. Rhodo. Mt. Holly Witch Hazel

Deep Creek

We are now on the Deep Creek Trail off Highway 441 just south of Newfound Gap. Our boots are the first to crunch through an 8-inch blanket of snow reflecting the blue sky on this beautiful but cold winter day. This spot is about a quarter-mile below the trail head on a steep, exposed north-facing slope.

We often see northern hardwood trees like yellow birch, buckeye and beech mixing in with the hemlock forest at this elevation (4700') on the North Carolina side. Many folks would call this a hemlock-northern hardwood forest with dominant hemlocks, and this would be appropriate.

The hemlocks here are large enough (27 inches) to be old enough to be considered virgin. Hemlock wooly adelgid is evident. On nearby south-facing exposed slopes, high elevation northern red oak forest can be found. Above this spot near the trailhead, red spruce-northern hardwood forest clothes the north-facing slope.

ELE.	DOM. CANOPY TREES	DISP. CANOPY TREES	SUB-CANOPY TREES	UNDER-STORY TREES & SHRUBS
4700'	Hemlock	Y. Birch Silverbell Sug.Maple Red Spruce	Beech	R. Rhodo.

Classic Cove Hardwood Forest

Forest Types Included from the Great Smoky Mountains National Park All Taxa Biodiversity Inventory (http://www.dlia.org/index.shtml):

Southern Appalachian Cove Forest (Typic Montane Type)
Southern Appalachian Cove Forest (Rich Montane Type)
Southern Appalachian Red Oak Cove Forest

ELE.	DOM. CANOPY TREES	DISP. CANOPY TREES	SUB-CANOPY TREES	UNDER-STORY TREES & SHRUBS
2500-4000'	Y. Poplar Basswood Silverbell W. Ash Red Maple	Sug. Maple Buckeye B. Birch Cuc-tree Hemlock B. Cherry N. Red Oak Bitt. Hick.	Usually thin Serviceberry Canopy tree saplings	Usually thin F. Dogwood Pepperbush R. Rhodo. Sweet-shrub Str. Maple

Forest Summary

- Found along streams and on north-facing, low protected slopes in the middle elevation zone.

- Canopy dominated by a <u>large number</u> of tree species including some mix of the following: yellow poplar, mountain silverbell, white basswood, white ash, red maple, sugar maple, yellow buckeye, black birch, Eastern hemlock.

- Yellow birch is absent or rarely dominant.
- Subcanopy and understory are usually thin.
- Herbaceous layer is usually very rich and diverse.

Forest Description

We apply the term "classic" in this book to the middle elevation cove hardwood forest to emphasize the outstanding character of this forest found only in the southern Appalachian Mountains and to distinguish it from the less unique low elevation river cove forest. Classic Cove hardwood forests are found between 2500 feet and 4000 feet elevation in coves along most of the Park's less acidic streams. Often the coves are narrow, rocky and steep. Middle elevation gaps like Cucumber Gap and flats also support classic cove hardwood forests.

There are pockets of virgin classic cove hardwood forest in many parts of the Park. Most occur in the northeastern section where the largest tracts of virgin forest of any kind in eastern America exist. The Greenbriar and upper Cosby Coves are access points for many of these magnificent forests. Also called the southern Appalachian cove forest, or simply the cove hardwood forest, the classic cove hardwood forest is the botanical wonderland of our Eastern forests. Nowhere else in eastern America exists a forest with such plant riches. Several reasons account for much of this diversity. During the last ice age plants and animals retreating from northern ice sheets found refuge in the southern Appalachian Mountains. Here trees from the north crowded in with trees from the south eventually forming new forest associations, some unique to these mountains.

Another reason for the richness of the classic cove hardwood forest is lack of disturbance. Though many of these higher coves were completely logged, most were not subjected to the intensive grazing and crop raising that occurred along lower elevation coves. As a result the rich herbaceous plant layer is fairly intact.

A third reason for the plant riches found here relates to ideal growing conditions. The combination of cooler summertime temperatures, ample rain, rich moist soil and protection from extremes of heat and cold by adjacent mountain slopes provides a made-to-order growing environment. Given enough time trees here can reach enormous proportions, and fortunately, the inaccessibility of these mountains has in many cases afforded the time.

The canopy of the classic cove hardwood forest is characteristically dominated by a large number of tree species sharing the canopy. The species mix can vary depending on site characteristics and history, but usually consists of some mix of the trees listed in the table above. An abundance of pioneer trees like yellow poplar, cucumbertree and black cherry usually indicates a younger forest than one where these three species are fewer in number, larger in size and accompanied by medium-size shade tolerant trees like basswood, hemlock and buckeye. Indeed, it may not be possible to account for all the different combinations of tree dominants these forests exhibit. Part of the excitement and wonder of entering the classic cove hardwood forest is discovering what mix of trees awaits the tree enthusiast. Few can emerge from such a forest without a sense of enrichment and a feeling of reverent awe.

Another characteristic aspect of the classic cove hardwood forest is its rich herbaceous plant layer. Subcanopy and understory trees are usually sparse allowing enough sunlight and moisture for a lush carpet of colorful wildflowers, grasses, sedges and ferns to flourish. Visualize yourself wandering through such a forest on a warm, sunny April afternoon with shafts of sunshine highlighting these forest beauties. Your dreams await you in GSMNP!

As you ascend toward 4000 feet especially on the North Carolina side of the main divide, cool cove forest trees begin to dominate the classic cove forest mix while lower elevation trees drop out. Yellow poplar, bitternut hickory and cucumbertree disappear. Basswood thins out while yellow birch and buckeye increase. Flowering dogwood, spicebush and sweetshrub drop out of the understory. Striped maple and alternate-leaf dogwood increase.

Examples of Classic Cove Hardwood Forests

Cucumber Gap
The Cucumber Gap Trail near Elkmont campground connects Jakes Creek and Little River spanning Cucumber Gap in the process. Elevation of the gap is about 3000 feet with surrounding

peaks reaching about 4000 feet. The forest here looks to be over a century old. The gap was no doubt named for the towering cucumbertrees, more numerous here than in other Park areas. The big silverbells are also impressive with their flaky reddish bark. Mountain folk called this tree "peawood" after the white pea-like flowers.

ELE	DOM. CANOPY TREES	DISP. CANOPY TREES	SUB-CANOPY TREES	UNDER-STORY TREES & SHRUBS
3000'	Y. Poplar Cuc-tree Silverbell Sug. Maple Red Maple Buckeye	Y. Birch Basswood B. Birch Hemlock N. Red Oak	Canopy Saplings	Mt. Holly Pepperbush Doghobble

Porters Creek Trail

Drive the narrow, windy road beside the Little Pigeon River in Greenbriar. Pass the Ramsey Cascades access road on the left, and you will end up at the parking lot for the Porters Creek and Brushy Mountain trails.

The combined trail begins as a wide, well-graded gravel road that ascends gradually past old stone walls surrounding forgotten home sites and cemeteries. At the trail fork, go left on the Porters Creek trail. Another quarter mile brings you to what some hikers call the "scary bridge", a long angled log bridge fairly high over Porters Creek. This is a great place to take a dip in summer if you can brave the crisp mountain water!

The bridge is the portal into a glorious classic cove hardwood forest. This is virgin forest with silverbells, basswoods, sugar maples and hemlocks in the 36-inch diameter range. The hemlock wooly adelgid has done its work here too. In late June, the ground is literally covered in places with curious round green ball-shaped fruit about 1/4-inch in diameter. I will leave you to figure out the tree from which they have fallen, but it has something to do with fish!

ELE.	DOM. CANOPY TREES	DISP. CANOPY TREES	SUB-CANOPY TREES	UNDER-STORY TREES & SHRUBS
2600'	Buckeye Silverbell Basswood	Hemlock Sugar Maple Poplar N. Red Oak	sparse	R. Rhodo. F. floor rich in wildflowers and ferns

Cook cabin site on Little Cataloochee Creek.
Once a bustling agricultural community specializing in apple orchards, the Little Cataloochee Creek watershed is now mostly forested. A few settlement buildings like the Cook cabin remain, and numerous stone foundations and low stone walls testify to former apple houses and pasture fences.

This plot is very poplar dominated. It should really be called an early succession yellow poplar forest, and is an example of the many forests of this kind in post-settlement Park areas. The largest poplars average about 20 inches dbh. Our poplar age equation (5 X dbh) gives an age estimate of around 100 years.

ELE.	DOM. CANOPY TREES	DISP. CANOPY TREES	SUB-CANOPY TREES	UNDER-STORY TREES & SHRUBS
3400'	Y. Poplar Red Maple	B. Cherry Sug. Maple	Silverbell	Str. Maple Hemlock sapling

Cool Cove Forest

Forest Types Included from the Great Smoky Mountains National Park All Taxa Biodiversity Inventory (http://www.dlia.org/index.shtml):

Southern Appalachian Northern Hardwood Forest
*   (Rich Type)*
Southern Appalachian Hardwood Boulderfield Forest
*   (Typic Type)*

ELE.	DOM. CANOPY TREES	DISP. CANOPY TREES	SUB-CANOPY TREES	UNDER-STORY TREES & SHRUBS
4000-4500'	Y. Birch Buckeye Sug. Maple Basswood	Beech B. Birch B. Cherry Silverbell	Red Maple	A. Dogwood Str. Maple R. Rhodo. Serviceberry

Forest Summary

- Found in coves on the North Carolina side of the Park between 4000 and 4500 feet elevation.

- Yellow buckeye, yellow birch, sugar maple and white basswood are the dominant canopy trees.

- Trees characteristic of the classic cove hardwood forest like yellow poplar are absent.

- Hobblebush, a shrub characteristic of the northern hardwood forest is usually absent.

- This forest often has a rich herbaceous layer similar to that of the classic cove hardwood forest.

Forest Description

Cool cove forests, considered by some as a subtype of the classic cove hardwood forest, occur between about 4000 and 4500 ' in elevation especially along south-facing stream channels. These landforms are more abundant on the North Carolina side of the main divide than on the Tennessee side. In Tennessee, the classic cove hardwood forest often transitions into the red spruce-northern hardwood forest at around 4000 ' elevation, skipping the cool cove forest in the process.

The cool cove forest occupies upper coves and ravines lined with narrow rocky streams that pitch and tumble down the mountain in cheerful audible ecstasy. It can also be found on some north-facing protected slopes. Where it occurs, it is a transition forest between the classic cove hardwood forest and the northern hardwood forest, and it harbors components of both forest types.

This is a cool moist place much of the year. Above 4000 feet, maintaining adequate soil moisture is no longer a problem. The weather is generally cooler here than down below in the classic cove hardwood forest, and the species mix reflects this. Yellow birch and yellow buckeye, diagnostic trees of the northern hardwood forest, dominate the canopy, but hobblebush, a characteristic shrub of the northern hardwood forest, is usually absent. Yellow poplar, cucumbertree, and bitternut hickory, all classic cove trees are absent up here, but basswood and sugar maple are usually present in the canopy. In contrast to the usually sparse understory of the classic cove hardwood forest, the cool cove understory supports striped maple, alternate-leaf dogwood, serviceberry and rhododendron.

Yellow birch is easily identified by its flaky golden bark. This tree found in cold places compensates the chilly hiker by providing some of the best firewood available. The yellow birch tree may have a reputation as a "cowboy" tree from its habit of germinating on fallen logs. The log provides organic matter as it decomposes, and when the process is complete yellow birch roots remain straddling the air like a bowlegged cowboy!

Black cherry trees up here above 4000 feet drop their cherries in late September and early October. This is handy for black bears fattening themselves up for winter. On a misty October morning a hiker in the cool cove forest is likely to be thrilled or perhaps chilled by the site of bear scat on the trail loaded with cherry seeds as well as those of the huckleberry bush.

Examples Of Cool Cove Forests

Oconaluftee River

Just after the first of the two big switchbacks heading north on highway 441 toward Newfound Gap, there is a pullout on the right. The old highway to the top (National Park Road) now just a wide trail runs off to the right where it crosses a little stream. Several large yellow buckeye and sugar maple trees dominate the canopy here along with smaller yellow birch and basswood. A 30-inch buckeye and a 36-inch sugar maple testify to the old status of this site. This is a climax forest, and it is either a virgin forest or a disturbed old-growth forest.

ELE.	DOM. CANOPY TREES	DISP. CANOPY TREES	SUB-CANOPY TREES	UNDER-STORY TREES & SHRUBS
4200'	Y. Birch Buckeye Sug. Maple	Basswood Hemlock	Red Maple	R. Rhodo.

Deep Creek

Follow the Deep Creek trail from 441, down to flowing water, about one half-mile from the trailhead. There is a 40-inch buckeye in this plot, and a whopping 22-inch Fraser magnolia! The disturbance map referred to in the Forest Disturbance chapter lists this area as virgin forest, and it appears to be.

The presence of basswood in the dominant canopy suggests this is a cool cove forest, but some folks would call it a northern hardwood forest, since it has beech, yellow birch and buckeye, the diagnostic species for northern hardwoods. The presence of beech sprouts, pin cherry and silverbell hint of the beech gap forest that might be found a little higher up on the exposed, south-facing slope.

This site is on the warmer south-facing, North Carolina side of the main Smokys divide. At this same elevation on the cooler Tennessee side, we would be surrounded by red spruce-northern hardwood forest. In Tennessee, red spruce follows streams down the mountain to about 4000 feet where classic cove hardwood forest takes over. Cool cove forest is usually absent.

Red spruce disappears from the Park southwest of Silers Bald leaving northern hardwood forests and high elevation northern red oak forests to clothe upper slopes in both Tennessee and North Carolina.

ELE.	DOM. CANOPY TREES	DISP. CANOPY TREES	SUB-CANOPY TREES	UNDER-STORY TREES & SHRUBS
4400'	Buckeye Basswood Y. Birch	Silverbell Hemlock	Fraser Mag. Pin Cherry	Beech sprouts

Mixed Oak-Hickory-Red Maple Forest

Forest Types Included from the Great Smoky Mountains National Park All Taxa Biodiversity Inventory (http://www.dlia.org/index.shtml):

Appalachian Montane Oak-Hickory Forest
        (Typic Acidic Type)
Appalachian Montane Oak - Hickory Forest
        (Low-Ele.Xeric Type)
Ridge-and-Valley Dry-Mesic White Oak - Hickory Forest

ELE.	DOM. CANOPY TREES	DISP. CANOPY TREES	SUB-CANOPY TREES	UNDER-STORY TREES & SHRUBS
1500-4000' Moist Sites	N. Red Oak W. Oak	Y. Poplar Hemlock Silverbell B. Birch	Fraser Mag.	F. Dogwood R. Rhodo.
	Chest. Oak	Blackgum M. Hick. Red Maple B. Locust White Pine	Sourwood	Serviceberry
Dry Sites	Scar. Oak Black Oak S. Red Oak	Pig. Hick. Va. Pine Pitch Pine		Mt. Laurel Chestnut sprouts

Forest Summary

- Found on protected slopes and ridgetops between 1500 and 3000 feet elevation.

- Found on exposed slopes and ridgetops between 3000 and 4000 feet elevation.

- Characterized by some mixture of oaks depending on site moisture, including northern red oak, white oak, chestnut oak and scarlet oak.

- Lowland oak species like black oak and southern red oak may be present.

- Red maple is relatively and temporarily abundant as an American chestnut replacement.

Forest Description

In the low elevation zone, the mixed oak-hickory-red maple forest occurs on protected slopes and protected ridgetops. In this zone, protection from the drying effects of hot sun is beneficial. This means north-facing protected slopes provide the most favorable environment for growth. Here northern red oak and white oak are likely to be the dominant oaks along with mockernut hickory. Hemlock may mix in with the oaks on these relatively moist sites. Red maple is likely to be more abundant also.

On hotter, dryer south-facing slopes scarlet and chestnut oaks are likely to be more common along with pignut hickory. White pine, black oak and southern red oak will probably show up on these dry, sites also.

In the middle elevation zone, the mixed oak-hickory-red maple forest occurs on exposed slopes and ridgetops. Though exposed, these landforms probably provide similar habitats to their lower elevation zone counterparts and would support similar species with the exception of white pine and southern red oak which are strictly low elevation zone trees.

Forest age has a lot to do with the tree species mix too, with early succession pioneer trees being more abundant in young forests. Yellow poplar is the main pioneer tree on moist sites, while black locust, Virginia pine and pitch pine are more common on early succession dry sites. As is frequently the case in the Park, a forest of two ages is often encountered. You may find a few huge oaks and hickories over one hundred years old surrounded by an early succession forest of smaller younger pioneer trees.

Oaks and hickories dominate the mixed oak-hickory-red maple forest when it reaches maturity (200-250 yrs). Red maple is prominent in these forests right now due to its role as a replacement tree for blight-killed American chestnut trees. Red maple is not long-lived like the oaks and hickories, so it will become much less important as these forests mature.

Above about 3000 feet elevation, the mixed oak-hickory-red maple forest becomes dominated more and more exclusively by one species of oak, depending on elevation and landform. Northern red oak dominates on higher cooler sites. Chestnut oak dominates lower, dryer locations, and white oak falls in between these extremes. Scarlet oak becomes scarce with increasing elevation. These forests eventually take on the name of their dominant oak.

Examples of Mixed Oak-Hickory-Red Maple Forest

West Prong Trail

Plot number 40 is located at 1700 ' elevation on a very steep east-facing protected slope along West Prong Trail. It is against the law for other than Park personnel to establish plot markers in the forest or disturb it in any way. This is absolutely necessary to maintain the natural integrity of the forest. Plot 40 is marked only on paper in my notebook. Its trees were left completely undisturbed by the plot-taking process.

This is a mature forest dominated by intermediate and shade tolerant trees. The oaks average 18 inches dbh. The red hickories average 11 inches. A 30- inch sweetgum probably began life as a pioneer tree in an opening associated with the William Walker settlement where the Tremont Institute now sits.

Red hickory, *Carya ovalis* is intermediate in characteristics between pignut hickory and mockernut hickory. Not recognized by all taxonomists, it is probably a hybrid between the other two hickories. The tendency of hickories to hybridize has given taxonomists difficulty, but every squirrel knows that mockernut produces the largest and tastiest nuts of the three species. Our squirrel also knows the much thicker mockernut shells are a little harder to penetrate than those of red hickory, and that pignut hickory nuts are small and not worth the trouble if better nuts are available.

ELE	DOM. CANOPY TREES	DISP. CANOPY TREES	SUB-CANOPY TREES	UNDER-STORY TREES & SHRUBS
1700	R. Hick. Red Maple Chest. Oak	Scar. Oak Y. Poplar Sweet gum	Sourwood Hemlock saplings	Umbrella Mag.

Chestnut Oak-Hickory-Red Maple Forest

Forest Types Included from the Great Smoky Mountains National Park All Taxa Biodiversity Inventory (http://www.dlia.org/index.shtml):

Appalachian Montane Oak Hickory Forest
(Chestnut Oak Type)
Chestnut Oak Forest (Mesic Slope Heath Type)
Chestnut Oak Forest (Xeric Ridge Type)
Chestnut Oak Forest (Mesic Slope Heath Type)

ELE	DOM. CANOPY TREES	DISP. CANOPY TREES	SUB-CANOPY TREES	UNDER-STORY TREES & SHRUBS
1500-3500'	Chest. Oak Pig. Hick. Red Maple	Scar. Oak Black Oak Silverbell W. Pine Blackgum Va. Pine B. Locust Pitch Pine Y. Poplar N. Red Oak	Sourwood Sassafrass	F. Dogwood. A. Chestnut sprouts R. Rhodo. Mt. Laurel

Forest Summary

- Found on exposed slopes and ridgetops between 1500 and 3500 feet elevation.
- Chestnut oak is the dominant oak in this forest.
- Red maple is relatively and temporarily more abundant as an American chestnut replacement.

Forest Description

The chestnut oak-hickory-red maple forest is found predominantly on exposed slopes in the low elevation zone and on exposed slopes and ridgetops in the middle elevation zone. American chestnut, once dominated these locations in the former American chestnut-chestnut oak forest. Chestnut oak and red maple have now replaced American chestnut, whose struggling root systems still cling to life in places. Sapling sprouts from the root systems often appear in the understory here, growing, even sometimes flowering, until the blight finds and fells them.

Exposed slopes and ridgetops are more often than not dry, nutrient-poor sites. Chestnut oak is well adapted to these conditions, and red maple's robust genetic complement allows it to adapt to a variety of conditions including those found here. Pignut hickory survives well on these dry sites and is much more common than its more demanding sib mockernut hickory, found in moister richer forests. At lower elevations, dry site oaks like scarlet and black oak accompany the canopy dominants. Up higher, northern red oak replaces them.

In the low elevation zone, an abundance of Virginia pine, black locust and yellow poplar in the canopy signifies a younger forest since these are shade intolerant pioneer trees. In the middle elevation zone, pitch pine becomes a more abundant pioneer tree on these sites.

On acidic sites rhododendron and mountain laurel may completely dominate the understory of the chestnut oak-hickory-red maple forest. This variation is sometimes referred to as the chestnut oak-heath forest because both rhododendron and mountain laurel are members of the acid-loving Heath family of plants. Sourwood, another Heath family member, is usually abundant in the heath forest too.

Examples of the Chestnut Oak-Hickory-Red Maple Forest

Bote Mountain
Take the Bote Mountain Trail southeast from Laurel Creek Road. After the West Prong Trail joins it, the trail turns south, following

the ascending ridgeline of Bote Mountain. This plot is located on a very steep, northwest-facing exposed slope just below the ridgeline. Pine beetle damage is fairly extensive here with dead Virginia pines evident. In contrast to the chestnut blight and hemlock wooly adelgid, pine beetles are a native pest, having thrived here as long as the pine species they attack.

On these dry nutrient-poor sites, pines are the pioneer trees ushering in the earliest stage of forest succession. As the pines age and weaken, pine beetles often attack, creating forest openings that chestnut oak and red maple take advantage of. The forest then transitions into the intermediate stage of forest succession. As succession advances further on this site, red maple will eventually be replaced by shade tolerant pignut hickory and hemlock.

ELE	DOM. CANOPY TREES	DISP. CANOPY TREES	SUB-CANOPY TREES	UNDER-STORY TREES & SHRUBS
1900'	Chest. Oak Red Maple	Pig. Hick. Hemlock Va. Pine	Sourwood	R. Rhodo. Mt. Laurel Huckleberry

Elkmont
Let's move over to a protected ridgetop above Elkmont Campground. I hike up here after breakfast while Jenny chats with the couple in the campsite next door. Corned beef hash (from the can) is my preferred camp breakfast. It is winter time and the grease coats chapped lips and hungry ribs. I can now feel the cholesterol-induced blood pressure surge that brings warmth to chilled bones!

One would expect this protected site, 500 feet higher in elevation and more protected to be a little cooler and moister than the Bote Mountain site. The presence of poplar and northern red oak and absence of pines suggests this is true.

Sassafras, a shade intolerant pioneer tree occupies the dispersed canopy (its characteristic position) on this site. There are many sassafras root sprouts in the understory also. The tree does not reproduce from seeds well, but it is a prolific sprouter, especially after fire. Normally, intolerant tree seedlings could not endure the shady understory, but these sprouts, connected to the mother tree have a source of nourishment that will probably ensure their survival.

Sassafras has experienced two ages; one of fame and another of infamy. In Colonial times its roots and bark were exported in quantity to Europe as a cure-all, especially for venereal disease, and as a tasty tea. One can imagine it as the official drink of the 17th-century brothel. More recently, sassafras tea has been proven to cause liver damage and cancer in laboratory animals. The obvious moral is; don't feed sassafras tea to your pet rodent! On a more serious note, this author grew up with a friend whose mother drank sassafras tea every day. A pot of it always simmered on her stove. She died at age 40 from stomach cancer, and I have always wondered if sassafras was the culprit.

ELE	DOM. CANOPY TREES	DISP. CANOPY TREES	SUB-CANOPY TREES	UNDER-STORY TREES & SHRUBS
2400'	Red Maple Chest. Oak	Sassafrass Hemlock N. Red Oak	Sourwood Fraser Mag.	R. Rhodo. Mt. Laurel

Northern Red Oak-Hickory-Red Maple Forest

Forest Types Included from the Great Smoky Mountains National Park All Taxa Biodiversity Inventory (http://www.dlia.org/index.shtml):

Appalachian Montane Oak - Hickory Forest (Red Oak Type)
Southern Appalachian Red Oak Cove Forest

ELE	DOM. CANOPY TREES	DISP. CANOPY TREES	SUB-CANOPY TREES	UNDER-STORY TREES & SHRUBS
2500 - 4500	N. Red Oak Red Maple Pig. Hick.	Y. Poplar B. Birch B. Locust M. Hick.	Sourwood Serviceberry Silverbell	Chestnut sprouts Str. Maple F. Dogwood Buffalo-nut

Forest Summary

- Found on protected and exposed slopes between about 3000 and 4500 feet elevation.

- Northern red oak is the dominant oak in this forest.

- Red maple is relatively and temporarily more abundant as an American chestnut replacement.

Forest Description

In GSMNP the northern red oak-hickory-red maple forest occupies protected and exposed slopes in the middle elevation zone. Between about 2500' and 4000' it grows on protected slopes. In these more favorable locations northern red oak is accompanied by less hickory and more of the classic cove hardwoods like silverbell, poplar, sugar maple and hemlock. Above 4000' elevation, it moves on to exposed slopes with hickories, red maple

114

and sourwood. American chestnut once strongly dominated exposed slopes along with northern red oak. Northern red oak and red maple have replaced the chestnut and so now they strongly dominate this forest type.

Examples of Northern Red Oak-Hickory-Red Maple Forests

Kephart Prong Trail
This site is located at 3700 feet elevation on a protected spur ridge just above the Kephart Prong backcountry shelter. It is more cove-like in its composition than the next example from an exposed slope. It is interesting to note that mountain silverbell joins up with northern red oak in the cove-like protected slope forests, follows it up on to exposed slopes and finally up into the high elevation northern red oak forest on exposed ridgetops at 5000 feet elevation.

ELE	DOM. CANOPY TREES	DISP. CANOPY TREES	SUB-CANOPY TREES	UNDER-STORY TREES & SHRUBS
3700 feet	N. Red Oak Red Maple	W. Ash B. Birch Hemlock	Silverbell Sug. Maple	Beech Mt. Holly Silverbell

Palmer Creek Trail
Hike the Palmer Creek Trail from Cataloochee Creek north to a gap at 3900' elevation. Little Cataloochee Creek is north of the gap. This plot is located on the exposed slope overlooking the gap. American chestnut sprouts testify to this tree's former dominance here.

ELE	DOM. CANOPY TREES	DISP. CANOPY TREES	SUB-CANOPY TREES	UNDER-STORY TREES & SHRUBS
4200'	N. Red Oak Red Maple	B. Birch Pig. Hick. Y. Poplar	Silverbell	Serviceberry A. chestnut Str. Maple

High Elevation Northern Red Oak Forest

Forest Types Included from the Great Smoky Mountains National Park All Taxa Biodiversity Inventory (http://www.dlia.org/index.shtml):

High-Elevation Red Oak Forest (Deciduous Shrub Type)
High-Elevation Red Oak Forest (Evergreen Shrub Type)
High-Elevation Red Oak Forest (Tall Herb Type)

ELE	DOM. CANOPY TREES	DISP. CANOPY TREES	SUB-CANOPY TREES	UNDER-STORY TREES & SHRUBS
4500'-5000' Dry, Acidic Sites	N. Red Oak (75%) of canopy	Y. Birch Red Maple B. Cherry	Sourwood	Witch Hazel Mt. Holly R. Rhodo Cat. Rhodo.. Mt. Laurel
4500'-5000' Moist, less acidic Sites	N. Red Oak (75%) of canopy	Y. Birch Red Maple Red Spruce Silverbell Beech	Pin. Cherry	Serviceberry Mt. Holly Str. Maple

Forest Summary

- Found on exposed ridgetops between 4500 and 5000 feet elevation.
- Northern red oak comprises 75% of the canopy.

Forest Description

In the southern Appalachians, especially south of the range of red spruce, northern red oak is a dominant tree in the 4500'-5000' elevation range on exposed slopes and ridgetops. Early researcher R. H. Whittaker identified two "races" of northern red oak in GSMNP and the southern Appalachians. The high elevation race of the ridgetop forests that Whittaker called "borealis" is better adapted to cold conditions than its low elevation counterpart.

On these exposed upper slopes and ridgetops, the northern red oak-hickory-red maple forest meets both the northern hardwood forest and the red spruce forest. Its ridgetop location is too nutrient-poor to be dominated by northern hardwoods, and too low in elevation to be dominated by red spruce, but it contains trees from all three forests, and northern red oak dominates.

Northern red oak comprises 75% or more of the canopy with red maple usually present. Other associates depend on how dry and acidic the site is. Dry, acidic sites usually have yellow birch and black cherry as dispersed canopy trees with Heath family members like sourwood, rosebay rhododendron, Catawba rhododendron and mountain laurel in the understory. On more moist, less acidic sites northern red oak may be accompanied by yellow birch, red maple, red spruce, mountain silverbell or American beech. Pin cherry is usually found in the subcanopy with Allegheny serviceberry, mountain holly and striped maple in the understory.

Examples of High Elevation Northern Red Oak Forest

Thomas Divide Trail
Thomas divide is a main ridge branching southward off the main divide of the Smokies just southwest of Newfound Gap. The high elevation northern red oak forest grows along the Thomas Divide Trail near its intersection with Newfound Gap Road (441) about 5 miles below Newfound Gap.

There are some giant northern red oaks in the canopy here. One measured 60 inches dbh with an estimated age of roughly 250 years. These big trees are obviously older than the trees in the dispersed canopy. It is likely loggers left the big red oaks when they cut this area perhaps 60 or 70 years ago.

The hemlock in this forest at 4900' elevation is about as high up as hemlock goes. Also striped maple will begin giving way to mountain maple above this elevation.

The many beech sprouts in the understory are probably the work of beech bark disease. First the disease kills the mature beech trees. This stimulates much beech sprout production in the understory. When the sprouts reach sapling size the disease returns to attack the sprouts usually killing the trees, roots and all, with its second passing.

ELE	DOM. CANOPY TREES	DISP. CANOPY TREES	SUB-CANOPY TREES	UNDER-STORY TREES & SHRUBS
4900', Ridgetops	N. Red Oak (75%) of canopy	Silverbell Red Maple Y. Birch Hemlock Red Spruce	Pin. Cherry	Str. Maple Beech sprouts

High Elevation White Oak Forest

Forest Types Included from the Great Smoky Mountains National Park All Taxa Biodiversity Inventory (http://www.dlia.org/index.shtml):

Southern Blue Ridge High-Elevation White Oak Forest

ELE	DOM. CANOPY TREES	DISP. CANOPY TREES	SUB-CANOPY TREES	UNDER-STORY TREES & SHRUBS
4000-4500'	White Oak	Sassafras Blackgum	A. Chestnut stump sprouts	Mt. Laurel

Forest Summary

- Found on exposed usually dry ridgetops between 4000 and 4500 feet elevation.
- White oak comprises 75% of the canopy.

Forest Description

The high elevation white oak forest occurs between about 4000 and 4500 feet elevation usually on the driest, poorest ridgetops as islands within forests dominated by northern red oak. Not abundant in the Park, this forest type is more common farther south where the highest peaks range between 4000 and 4500 feet.

White oak makes up at least 50 % of the canopy. The trees are often stunted and twisted having been shaped by wind and ice. The picturesque but unmarketable shapes thus created have usually saved the oaks from the logger's saw, resulting in their occurrence as virgin or old-growth forests.

Forest Examples

Kelly's Knob

This example is from outside the Smokies, but it is fairly representative of the forest type. Kelly's Knob is a dry nutrient-poor exposed ridgetop. Located along the Appalachian Trail south of Dicks Creek Gap, it is one of Georgia's higher peaks.

Spruce-fir forest and northern hardwoods are lacking in these Georgia mountains where the state's highest summit, Brasstown Bald ascends to only 4784 feet above sea level. The high elevation northern red oak forest usually dominates the moister richer ridges here, with high elevation white oak forests more common on dryer poorer sites.

The low canopy of gnarled old white oaks on this site is orchard-like and picturesque. Scattered among the oaks are outcrops of what looks like granite gneiss, an intrusive metamorphic rock. Sand, a major weathering product of this rock type, forms soil lacking in nutrients and moisture holding ability.

The rocks and laurel on Kelly's Knob have conspired to create visual compositions that appear contrived. A perfect stone bench adorned with rock tripe lichen is over-arched by a single twisted mountain laurel. Late afternoon sunlight guilds the scene, transforming it into a place seemingly provided by the Creator for quiet contemplation of His work.

ELE	DOM. CANOPY TREES	DISP. CANOPY TREES	SUB-CANOPY TREES	UNDER-STORY TREES & SHRUBS
4300'	White Oak	B. Birch Black Oak Pig. Hick.	A. Chestnut stump sprouts Sourwood Serviceberry	Mt. Laurel

Oak-Pine Forest

Forest Types Included from the Great Smoky Mountains National Park All Taxa Biodiversity Inventory (http://www.dlia.org/index.shtml):

Southern Appalachian White Pine Forest
Appalachian White Pine - Xeric Oak Forest
Appalachian Shortleaf Pine Forest
Virginia Pine Successional Forest
Appalachian Low-Elevation Mixed Pine / Hillside Blueberry Forest

ELE	DOM. CANOPY TREES	DISP. CANOPY TREES	SUB-CANOPY TREES	UNDER-STORY TREES & SHRUBS
1500 - 2500'	Va. Pine Short. Pine Scar. Oak Chest. Oak Red Maple	White Pine Blackgum B. Locust Pig. Hick. Black Oak W. Oak	Sourwood Sassafras A. Chestnut sprouts	Mt. Laurel Blueberries (*Vaccinium spp.*) F. Dogwood
2500 - 4000'	Pitch Pine Tm. Pine Scarlet Oak Chest. Oak Red Maple	Blackgum B. Locust Pig. Hick.	Sourwood Sassafras A. Chestnut Sprouts	Mt. Laurel F. Dogwood

Forest Summary
- Found on dry exposed upper slopes and ridgetops between 1500 and 3500 feet elevation.

- Dry-site oaks like scarlet oak and chestnut oak along with pines including Virginia pine, shortleaf pine, white pine, pitch pine and table-mountain pine dominate the forest canopy.

- On sites where fires are excluded, oaks are becoming more dominant.

- On sites where burning is allowed (or practiced), pines remain dominant in the canopy.

- Forests where prescribed burning is practiced may be more aptly named, pine-oak forests.

Forest Description

In pre-park times, Cherokee Indians and early settlers burned dry exposed slopes and ridgetops regularly. Research has shown these sites burned on average about every 10 to 15 years. Burning cleared the forest of understory vegetation making hunting and travel easier. It stimulated production of sprouts, berries and acorns, foods both Indians and game animals relished. Pines and dry site oaks are fire resistant trees favored by fire. The thick bark of pines protects them from damage during low intensity ground fires, and dry site oaks like scarlet, black and chestnut oak readily re-sprout after fire injury.

Ground fires burned away the leaf litter exposing mineral soil, the perfect seed bed for wind blown pine seeds. The seedlings of fire sensitive trees like red maple and sourwood were eliminated resulting in numerous forest openings favorable for pine and oak seedling growth. These conditions created forests where pines were perpetuated as the climax forest canopy dominants. Ecologists call forests where the normal course of forest succession is foreshortened and held stationary by restrictive environmental conditions, edaphic climax forests.

With the Park's establishment in the 1930's, fires were suppressed. This allowed forest succession to proceed on these sites, albeit slowly. Time has witnessed the succession of most of these pine forests into oak-pine forests where dry site oaks and other dry site trees like black gum, sourwood and pignut hickory are replacing pine in the canopy.

In 1996 the National Park Service began a program of prescribed burning in Park areas once supporting edaphic climax pine forests. They also adopted a wildland fire use policy that allows lightening-caused fires to burn naturally in appropriate Park areas. Today, about 9 percent (45000 acres) of the Park's forests are considered pine dominated forests. The vast majority of these forests are in the southwestern part of the Park with large sections on lower Eagle, Hazel and Forney creeks and in the lower Abrams Creek watershed. We should probably call these forests pine-oak forests since prescribed burning will continue to give pines the upper hand here.

Elevation has an important effect on the kinds of pines and oaks that dominate oak-pine forests in GSMNP. In the low elevation zone (1500-2500') Virginia and shortleaf pines predominate with scarlet and black oaks as associates. Between 2500' and 3500' pitch and table-mountain pines are dominate, and above 3500' table-mountain pine remains as the dominant pine. Chestnut oak and white oak are the common associates here.

Formerly, American chestnut made up about 10 percent of the canopy in oak-pine forests. Since the chestnut blight, chestnut oak and red maple have replaced it on these dry nutrient-poor sites. Forest succession will proceed slowly on oak-pine sites where burning is excluded. Chestnut oak and white oak will likely remain into the climax forest. Red maple will be initially important in the canopy but drop out by about year 150, its average life span. White pine and pignut hickory are long-lived trees that will remain well into the climax forest stage.

Forest Examples

Bote Mountain Trail
From Laurel Creek Road the Bote Mountain Trail heads up the west flank of Bote Mountain arriving near the ridgetop where the West Prong Trail intersects at about 2000' elevation. This is an oak-pine site where fires are excluded, but it looks like the southern pine beetle, a native insect has taken its toll on the pines hastening the site's conversion to a forest where scarlet oak, red maple, pignut hickory and white pine will eventually dominate. The presence of black birch and hemlock is a bit confusing, but

nature has probably done this just to keep us on our toes and guessing, a refreshing predicament!

ELE	DOM. CANOPY TREES	DISP. CANOPY TREES	SUB-CANOPY TREES	UNDER-STORY TREES & SHRUBS
2000'	Va. Pine Short. Pine Red Maple	Scar. Oak W. Pine Pig. Hick.	Sourwood B. Birch saplings Hemlock saplings	Mt. Laurel F. Dogwood

Cataloochee Creek

The Palmer Cemetery is located at 2700 feet on a fairly protected south-facing slope overlooking Cataloochee Creek. After viewing the cemetery, Jenny and I put in a plot nearby. The trees appear to be about a century old. White pine is the dominant tree here as in other places in Cataloochee Valley. Red maple is also dominant here. This site is really a mixed oak-hickory-red maple forest with a bunch of white pine in it.

ELE	DOM. CANOPY TREES	DISP. CANOPY TREES	SUB-CANOPY TREES	UNDER-STORY TREES & SHRUBS
2700'	W. Pine Red Maple W. Oak	Scar. Oak Chest. Oak Pig. Hick.	Sourwood	Mt. Laurel

Northern Hardwood Forest

Forest Types Included from the Great Smoky Mountains National Park All Taxa Biodiversity Inventory (http://www.dlia.org/index.shtml):

Southern Appalachian Northern Hardwood Forest
        (Typic Type)
Blue Ridge Hemlock - Northern Hardwood Forest

ELE '	DOM. CANOPY TREES	DISP. CANOPY TREES	SUB-CANOPY TREES	UNDER-STORY TREES & SHRUBS
4500 - 5000	Y. Birch Buckeye Beech	Hemlock Sug. Maple B.Cherry N. Red Oak Silverbell	Sparse with mostly younger canopy trees.	Beech sprouts Mt. Maple A. Dogwood Str. Maple Hobblebush Mt. Holly Serviceberry

Forest Summary

- Found on creek flats, slopes and ridgetops between 4000 and 5000 feet elevation.
- Yellow birch, yellow buckeye, American beech are diagnostic canopy trees.
- Red spruce is absent or rare in the canopy.
- Basswood is absent or rare
- Hobblebush is common.
- Mountain ash is absent.

- More common on North Carolina side of GSMNP, and both sides south of the range of red spruce.

- Beech bark disease is reducing the role of American beech in this forest type.

Forest Description

The northern hardwood forest is found in upper stream coves, on upper protected slopes and exposed slopes mostly between 4500' and 5000' elevation. Within the geographic range of red spruce, the northern hardwood forest is more common on warmer south-facing slopes, like those on the North Carolina side. On cooler north-facing slopes like those on the Tennessee side, red spruce mixes with northern hardwoods to form the red spruce-northern hardwood forest. Southwest of Silers Bald, where red spruce no longer occurs, the northern hardwood forest is common on north and south-facing exposed slopes on both sides of the main divide above 4500 feet elevation.

Though American beech, yellow birch, yellow buckeye forests of GSMNP are called northern hardwood forests, they are significantly different from the true northern hardwood forests found further north. The true northern hardwood forest ranges from southern Canada down through New England and New York State, thence over to the Great Lakes and Minnesota. Its key indicator trees are sugar maple, yellow birch, American beech, striped maple and hobblebush. Some white pine and hemlock also occur. The northern hardwood forest lacks yellow buckeye as a key component. It includes white pine which is completely absent from the high elevation forests of the Smokies. These differences render the two forests distinct from each other, but the name has stuck to our southern Appalachian forests so we will use it to avoid further confusion.

Yellow birch and yellow buckeye are the diagnostic species of the Park's northern hardwood forests. American beech, once an abundant canopy tree here has in great part succumbed to the ravages of beech bark disease, resulting in its relegation to the understory where its spouts are often abundant.

Eastern hemlock is a dominant canopy tree in northern hardwood forests on steep slopes, especially on the warmer North Carolina side of the Park. We can call this the hemlock-northern hardwood forest, and consider it a transitional forest, where the acid cove-hemlock forest and the northern hardwood forest meet. The Forest

126

Finder (page 35) depicts this transition zone at around 4700 feet elevation, and this is where we find it on the North Carolina side. On the cooler Tennessee side, it occurs as low as 4000 feet.

The northern hardwood forest differs from the spruce-fir forest higher up by the absence of those two trees in the canopy and the absence of mountain ash in the subcanopy. The rarity of basswood and the presence of hobblebush distinguish this forest from the cool cove forest down lower.

American beech is found growing from the hot coastal plains of Florida up to the icy Appalachian ridgetops at 6000 feet elevation. How does a tree accommodate such a wide range of environmental conditions? According to R. H. Whittaker, prominent tree researcher, the American beech tree actually has 3 distinct genetic populations. Each population is adapted to a different elevation range. The white population is the lowland beech found in the Coastal Plain and in the Piedmont Plateau Province ranging up to about 2500 feet elevation. The red beech is found in the classic cove hardwood forest and other sites between about 3500 and 4500 feet. Above this the gray beech dominates giving unique character to the northern hardwood forest and the beech gap forest there.
.

Both northern red oak and white oak have also adopted this strategy for coping with the wide elevation range presented by the southern Appalachian Mountains, though each has only two distinct populations. High elevation northern red oak is called the borealis population, while the high elevation white oak population has been noted but not yet named. In general, high elevation populations of all three trees have a slightly different appearance than their lowland counterparts.

Another way trees cope with extreme environmental variations is by developing multiple chromosome sets. Most organisms have two chromosome sets containing the genetic material dictating the organism's form and function. This is termed diploidy. Red maple, the most widely occurring tree in eastern North America has multiple chromosome sets, called polyploidy. Presumably, the additional genetic material enhances the tree's ability to adapt to a variety of environmental conditions

Examples of Northern Hardwood Forest

Alum Cave Bluffs Trail

The Alum Cave trail, branches from highway 441 about 4 miles north of Newfound Gap. It is one of the most heavily hiked trails in GSMNP. Even in dismal weather a few vehicles can be found in the parking lot. On sunny days, dozens of vehicles jam the parking lot and adjacent roadside. Walker Camp Prong and Alum Cave Creek join at the trailhead to form the headwaters of the West Prong of Pigeon River.

The trail interpretive brochure calls this a hemlock-northern hardwood forest. Indeed, it is a grand example of several forests joining together to create an interesting mix. The mixture likely results from three circumstances. First, the temperature-moisture regime provides suitable habitat for several forest types. The red spruce-northern hardwood forest, the classic cove hardwood forest and the acid cove-hemlock forest converge here. Second, the acidic rocks of the Anakeesta Formation result in acidic soils that favor hemlock and Heath family members like rhododendron. Finally, the fact that this is a virgin forest means shade tolerant trees from the several forest types like hemlock, beech and sugar maple have had plenty of growing time to become the dominant trees here.

ELE	DOM. CANOPY TREES	DISP. CANOPY TREES	SUB-CANOPY TREES	UNDER-STORY TREES & SHRUBS
3800 feet	Hemlock Y. Birch	B. Birch Sug. Maple Beech	Beech Red Spruce	R. Rhodo. Str. Maple

128

Heintooga Ridge Road

Take the Blue Ridge Parkway east from Oconaluftee to its intersection with Heintooga Ridge Road. A nearby gravel road follows Wolf Laurel Branch downstream. This plot was recorded a quarter-mile down the road and about 50 vertical feet above the stream. Chilly winds, clouds and mist shroud the peaks on this May day so very full of wildflowers and mountain wonder! Here I met Harry, an adventurous loner from New York City. I wish him well in his quest to visit all 50 states by his fiftieth birthday.

It is good to see some fairly big beech trees that appear healthy, though there are numerous, suspicious looking beech sprouts in the understory. A 46" yellow birch rules this plot! Upstream from this plot, red spruce appears in the canopy, but here it is absent. Downstream, yellow buckeye becomes more abundant.

ELE	DOM. CANOPY TREES	DISP. CANOPY TREES	SUB- CANOPY TREES	UNDER- STORY TREES & SHRUBS
4800 feet	Y. Birch	Beech Sug. Maple Buckeye	Sug. Maple	Str. Maple Beech Hobblebush

Red Spruce-Northern Hardwood Forest

Forest Types Included from the Great Smoky Mountains National Park All Taxa Biodiversity Inventory (http://www.dlia.org/index.shtml):

Red Spruce - Northern Hardwood Forest (Herb Type)
Red Spruce - Northern Hardwood Forest (Shrub Type)

ELE	DOM. CANOPY TREES	DISP. CANOPY TREES	SUB-CANOPY TREES	UNDER-STORY TREES & SHRUBS
4000 - 5000'	Red Spruce Y. Birch Buckeye	Beech Pin Cherry Red Maple	Fraser fir	Hobblebush Mt. Holly Mt. Maple R. Rhodo. Serviceberry Fraser Fir Highbush Blueberry A. Dogwood

Forest Summary

- Similar to northern hardwood forest, except more common on the Tennessee side.
- Red spruce is a dominant canopy member.

Forest Description

The red spruce-northern hardwood forest grows between about 4000' and 5000' elevation along north-facing creek channels and on north-facing slopes. These cooler moister landforms are more often found on the Tennessee side of the main divide of the Smokies than on the North Carolina side.

If you follow the creek upstream above 5000' elevation, spruce-fir forest takes over. Yellow buckeye and beech drop out of the mix, and Fraser fir becomes more abundant. If you follow the creek downstream below 4000' elevation you are likely to encounter either cool cove forest or the classic cove hardwood forest. Red spruce drops out, while basswood, yellow poplar and others appear.

Examples of Red Spruce-Northern Hardwood Forest

Road Prong Trail

The Road Prong trail begins on the road to Clingmans Dome, highest point in the Park. From the trailhead at about 5300 feet, the trail descends rapidly down a steep rocky slope to join the Road Prong, a chilly, foaming high mountain cascade. The trail parallels the stream, crossing it at intervals until it descends into the classic cove hardwood forest zone at about 4000 feet.

There are some big old yellow birch trees here above two feet in diameter. One ancient and twisted veteran measures 60 inches. Here is a 20 inch yellow buckeye and there a 28 inch red spruce. This is a virgin forest on the Tennessee side of the main divide. During early settlement days, the only access road across the main divide followed this trail. Before that, it was an ancient Indian path. What thoughts passed through the minds of those dusky travelers so far back in time when this spot was surrounded by millions of acres of primeval wilderness, home of bears, wolves and panthers?

ELE	DOM. CANOPY TREES	DISP. CANOPY TREES	SUB-CANOPY TREES	UNDER-STORY TREES & SHRUBS
5000 feet	Red Spruce Y. Birch Buckeye	Beech Pin Cherry Red Maple	Fraser fir	Hobblebush Mt. Holly Mt. Maple R. Rhodo. A. Dogwood

West Prong Pigeon River

Follow 441 heading north from Newfound Gap. Just after you complete the head part of the big dinosaur-shaped switchback, the Walker Camp Prong joins the road, flowing beside it. The elevation here is about 4300 feet, a great place for a prong side tree plot.

Red spruce really descends surprisingly low down the mountain on the Tennessee side. Over on the North Carolina side at 4300 feet along streams, we often find either cool cove forest or classic cove hardwood forest. On the Tennessee side, red spruce mixes in along the West Prong of Pigeon River as far down as the Alum Cave Bluffs Trail head at 3800 feet elevation.

ELE	DOM. CANOPY TREES	DISP. CANOPY TREES	SUB-CANOPY TREES	UNDER-STORY TREES & SHRUBS
4300 feet	Red Spruce Y. Birch Hemlock	Buckeye Pin Cherry	sparse, tree saplings	R. Rhodo. dominates the understory

Beech Gap Forest

Forest Types Included from the Great Smoky Mountains National Park All Taxa Biodiversity Inventory (http://www.dlia.org/index.shtml):

Southern Appalachian Beech Gap (North Slope Tall Herb Type)
Southern Appalachian Beech Gap (South Slope Sedge Type)

ELE.	DOM. CANOPY TREES	DISP. CANOPY TREES	SUB-CANOPY TREES	UNDER-STORY TREES & SHRUBS
4500-5500 feet	Beech	Silverbell Y. Birch Buckeye	Str. Maple	----------

Forest Summary

- Found as islands on exposed slopes between 4500 and 5500 feet elevation.
- Stunted American beech comprises 75% of the canopy.
- Beech bark disease and feral hogs have decimated this forest type.

Forest Description

The beech gap forest occurs in pockets on exposed slopes and in gaps between 4500 and 5000 feet elevation. Stunted American beech trees form the low canopy of this forest. On north-facing slopes yellow birch and yellow buckeye are the beech's associates though in lesser numbers than the beeches. On south-facing slopes mountain silverbell accompanies beech more commonly in what is sometimes called the "classic" beech gap forest.

Beech gap forests occur only in the southern Appalachian Mountains and they are increasingly rare here. Beech bark disease has killed most of the beech trees now, opening up the

133

forest floor to sun-loving plants like smooth blackberry that have choked out the once rich complement of ferns, wildflowers and sedges. Introduced European wild boar too have taken their toll on these plants. Formerly herbaceous plants including intermediate wood fern (*Dryopteris intermedia*), Appalachian white snakeroot (*Ageratina altissima*), Appalachian Heartleaf Aster (*Eurybia chlorolepis*) and on south-facing slopes Pennsylvania sedge (*Carex pensylvanica*) formed a thick lovely herbaceous stratum below the beeches. Unfortunately this forest community will likely become extinct in the near future.

Examples of Beech Gap Forests

Appalachian Tail

Take the Appalachian Trail, heading north from the Road Prong Trailhead on the Clingmans Dome Road. This beech gap forest is about a half mile up the trail.

This example of a beech gap forest has been protected from the ravages of wild hogs by hog exclosure fences; thus it seems fairly intact. Stunted beeches comprise the canopy along with a few red spruce and one or two yellow birches. We found several wind-thrown red spruces in and near this plot, testimony to the wind power up here on the top of the Eastern world. One thrown spruce had about 160 growth rings 25 feet from the tree base.

ELE.	DOM. CANOPY TREES	DISP. CANOPY TREES	SUB-CANOPY TREES	UNDER-STORY TREES & SHRUBS
5500 feet	Beech	Red Spruce Yellow Birch	-----	Beech sprouts with sedges below

Spruce-Fir Forest

Forest Types Included from the Great Smoky Mountains National Park All Taxa Biodiversity Inventory (http://www.dlia.org/index.shtml):

Red Spruce - Fraser Fir Forest (Deciduous Shrub Type)
Red Spruce - Fraser Fir Forest (Evergreen Shrub Type)
Red Spruce - Fraser Fir Forest (Hemlock Type)
Red Spruce Forest (Protected Slope Type)

ELE	DOM. CANOPY TREES	DISP. CANOPY TREES	SUB-CANOPY TREES	UNDER-STORY TREES & SHRUBS
5000-6000 feet	Red Spruce Y. Birch Fraser Fir (formerly)	Pin Cherry Red Maple	Mt. Ash Fraser Fir	Hobblebush Mt. Holly Mt. Maple R. Rhodo. Serviceberry Fraser Fir Highbush Blueberry A. Dogwood Minnibush

Forest Summary

- Found on all landforms between 5000 and 6000 feet elevation.
- Red spruce, Fraser fir and yellow birch comprise the dominant canopy.
- Pin cherry is usually present.
- Mountain ash is usually present.
- Hobblebush is usually present.
- Yellow buckeye is absent.
- The balsam wooly adelgid is reducing the role of Fraser fir in this forest type.

Forest Description

The spruce-fir forest grows on all landforms between 5000 and 6000 ' elevation in GSMNP, although Fraser fir is usually sparse in this forest below 5500 feet. In the high elevation zone (4500'-6600'), elevation exerts a stronger influence on forest composition than landform. Consequently, this forest is found with minor variations in ravines both wet and dry and on slopes and ridgetops.

Researchers have found that spruce-fir forests don't always grow back in areas where logging occurred. On warmer south-facing slopes, which are more abundant on the North Carolina side of the main divide, spruce-fir forests failed to grow back as low down on mountain slopes as did pre-logging spruce-fir forests. Clearcut logging results in significant soil loss from the slopes. This reduces the site's ability to provide the cool moist conditions necessary for spruce-fir forests to survive. This means you will find more spruce-fir forest and more red spruce-northern hardwood forest on the cooler Tennessee side of the main divide.

The Clingmans Dome Road provides outstanding access to the spruce-fir forest. It intersects with Highway 441 at Newfound Gap at about 5000' elevation and ends at the Clingmans Dome parking lot at 6300 feet. Though most of the north side of Clingmans Dome was logged by Little River Lumber Company before 1930, the peak of the main divide here and the south side support mostly virgin spruce-fir forest.

The spruce-fir forest is a place of contrasts. On one of the many moist cloudy summer days, the forest is dark and somber with needles dripping from a recent shower and mist fragments sifting through the trees. Then the sun breaks through into a brilliant blue sky revealing drifts of wildflowers in openings along the trail. August coaxes from the rocky ground patches of bee balm, white snakeroot, Joe pye weed and wild golden-glow. Bright orange hobblebush berries satisfy the eye, plump highbush blueberries both eye and appetite. The clear air brings a balsam-scented mountain breeze to refresh the hiker.

Winter is a time when mighty winds thrown halfway across the continent hammer the ancient spruces and birches in a battle of titans. Snow blankets the land. Ice sheathes frigid branches, and bone-cracking frosts penetrate deep into wood, rock and flesh, but breathtaking beauty remains, warming the heart, inspiring the mind.

Red spruce is now the dominant tree in this forest. Its arrow-straight trunk 15, 20 and 30 inches in diameter pierces the sky with a narrow crown of blackish-green needles. You will find large wind thrown spruces more common in the forest now. The Fraser firs that helped protect them from strong winds are gone. One such spruce cut from the trail displayed 175 growth rings at a point formerly about 12 feet off the ground.

Yellow birch is the most common hardwood tree in the spruce-fir forest, sharing the canopy with spruce. It also reaches massive size, wearing its advanced age with an air of picturesque dignity. Pin cherry is less abundant than spruce and birch. Also called fire cherry for its tendency to colonize burned areas, its shiny bronze trunk seems to glow like fire in the half-light of the understory.

Once dominant in the canopy of the spruce-fir forest, especially above 5500 feet, Fraser fir is now present only in the subcanopy and understory as seedlings too young to develop the bark fissures that allow the Balsam wooly adelgid lethal entry. By about age 20, the firs have developed bark fissures and are attacked, producing one or two crops of seeds before succumbing. The stark gray trunks of dead virgin firs are now a distinctive characteristic of the high country easily seen from any of the viewing points along the road.

Mountain ash, a tree not found much below 5000' feet grows in the subcanopy up here and is characteristic of the spruce-fir forest. A member of the rose family, its berries provide food for birds and bears. It is often crowded by young Fraser fir saplings thriving thick and green until the adelgid can fell them.

The demise of the Fraser firs left openings now crowded with understory trees, shrubs and herbs. Mountain maple and hobblebush are two high elevation understory plants not common in the woods below 5000' elevation.

Examples of Spruce-fir Forests

Appalachian Trail

From Newfound Gap parking lot hit the Appalachian Trail heading south. About a mile or so out you will encounter the place where this plot and a trail lunch were completed. Jenny likes bread sticks and dip. I go with Vienna sausages and Debbie cakes which contain the 4 major food groups-sugar, salt, fat and preservatives. What a contrast!

This site is an exposed ridgetop, slicing the cool thin air at 5500 ' above sea level. It is virgin forest. Balsam wooly adelgid is evident here. American beech is more common on these exposed slopes and ridges than it is in the more protected ravines, but beech bark disease may eventually make this distinction mute.

ELE	DOM. CANOPY TREES	DISP. CANOPY TREES	SUB-CANOPY TREES	UNDER-STORY TREES & SHRUBS
5500 '	Red Spruce Y. Birch	Fraser Fir Beech	Mt. Ash Fraser fir Pin Cherry	Hobblebush Mt. Holly Mt. Maple Fraser Fir

Noland Divide Trail

Follow the Noland Divide Trail from Clingmans Dome Road. Take the right fork in the trail that heads over to an abandoned water pumping station that once supplied water to the Clingmans Dome area. In route you also may ask what the microwave tower is doing here! It is a great place to make a cell phone call. Way up here at 5600 feet, the headwaters of Noland Creek are flowing to beat the band. At this elevation we would normally expect a dry ravine, but the 6643-foot meta-sandstone massif of Clingmans Dome provides enough watershed for a gushing creek.

Right now (August), shoulder-high mountain wildflowers of every color choke the trail. Scarlet bee balm, rose-colored turtleheads, white snakeroot, yellow and green wild goldenglow, purple Joe Pye weed. Bear tracks and scat are also abundant. We trespass through their blueberry and blackberry larder to establish a plot in this ancient virgin forest.

American beech is absent from the forest, perhaps preferring lower, warmer regions. Rhododendron is sparse but surviving. It has probably followed the stream up to the limits of its elevation range. Yellow buckeye is also absent. Its presence below 5000 feet marks the upper limit of the northern hardwood forest.

ELE	DOM. CANOPY TREES	DISP. CANOPY TREES	SUB-CANOPY TREES	UNDER-STORY TREES & SHRUBS
5600 '	Red Spruce Y. Birch	Pin Cherry	Mt. Ash	Hobblebush R. Rhodo. Fraser Fir Highbush Blueberry Mt. Maple

Fraser Fir Forest

Forest Types Included from the Great Smoky Mountains National Park All Taxa Biodiversity Inventory (http://www.dlia.org/index.shtml):

Fraser Fir Forest (Deciduous Shrub Type)
Fraser Fir Forest (Evergreen Shrub Type)

ELE	DOM. CANOPY TREES	DISP. CANOPY TREES	SUB-CANOPY TREES	UNDER-STORY TREES & SHRUBS
6000 - 6643 feet	Fraser Fir	Red Spruce Y. Birch Pin Cherry	Mt. Ash	N-Facing Slopes: Hobblebush Fraser Fir seedlings S-Facing Slopes: Cat. Rhodo. R. Rhodo. Car. Rhodo.

Forest Summary

- Found on all topographic positions above 6000 feet elevation.
- The balsam wooly adelgid has decimated this forest.

Forest Description

The Fraser fir forest forms islands in the high country above 6000 feet elevation. Fraser fir trees comprise 75% of the canopy, but the balsam wooly adelgid has destroyed most of the mature fir trees in this increasingly rare forest type.

On north-facing slopes, the understory of the Fraser fir forest is usually sparse, but it can support hobblebush and Fraser fir seedlings. On south-facing slopes, several species of Rhododendron often form a high, thick understory.

Eighteen thousand years ago the last surge of the Pleistocene ice age gripped the world. The southern Appalachian Mountains provided a corridor of escape and a place of refuge for plant and animal species "fleeing" ice-bound climates further north. These life forms would otherwise have suffered extinction, as did many European species whose southern escape route was blocked by east-west mountain chains draped in sheets of glacial ice.

The mountainous terrain of the southern Appalachians provided suitable habitats for many of the plant and animal refugees from the north, and they mixed with existing life forms to create ecological communities rich in species diversity. GSMNP was created to help protect these unique plant and animal associations so future generations can love them and learn from them.

With retreat of the ice about 10000 years ago, plants and animals migrated back along the mountains to repopulate the north. Balsam fir was one of these refugees. After its return north, continued warming separated it into a large northern population and a smaller southern population restricted to the high peaks of the southern Appalachians. Cut off from the larger northern population, the southern population became the distinct species we know as Fraser fir.

Examples of Fraser Fir Forest

Clingmans Dome Trail

Clingmans Dome parking lot is 6300' above sea level. The dome itself rises 6643', highest point in the Park and third highest east of the Mississippi River. A thick stand of young Fraser fir seedlings near the trail head grabs your attention as soon as the incredible view lets go of it. The parents of these young trees remain only as bare gray trunks dotting the landscape. They contrast with the vibrant green of the young seedlings, symbolizing both despair and hope in the battle against foreign pests like the balsam wooly adelgid.

To the left of the trail, a thicket of thornless blackberry bushes, hobblebush, highbush blueberries, wildflowers and grasses clothes the slopes with a pleasing array of textures and colors. It is August, and the blueberry bushes of nearby Andrews Bald are loaded. We will visit them when we are done here. Are bears thinking the same thing?

The tower at the top provides an awesome panorama of 5 states on clear days. It is breathtaking, but it reveals the extent of damage done by the adelgid. A forest of dead Fraser firs radiates out from the tower for several miles. Beyond this, however, the green folds of the mountains flow boldly in ranks, fading into blue as they merge with the sky. It looks much like it did before the dawn of the age of man when wild nature alone ruled what Horace Kephart referred to as God's unimproved creation.

ELE	DOM. CANOPY TREES	DISP. CANOPY TREES	SUB-CANOPY TREES	UNDER-STORY TREES & SHRUBS
6300-6643'	Fraser Fir seedlings Red Spruce	Pin Cherry	Mt. Ash,	Hobblebush Fraser Fir seedlings Thornless blackberry Highbush Blueberry

CHAPTER 10. TREE DESCRIPTIONS

Canopy Trees

TREE PAGES

Green Ash (*Fraxinus pennsylvanica*)
White Ash (*Fraxinus americana*)

<u>Frequency Abbreviations:</u>
C = Common (dominates the canopy with two or fewer associates)
F = Frequent (in the dominant canopy)
O = Occasional (frequently in dispersed canopy)
I = Infrequent (infrequent in dispersed canopy)
R=Rare

Occurrence

Low Elevation Zone (1500'-2500')

River Cove Forest-*G ash (I), W ash(I)*
Acid Cove-Hemlock Forest-*W ash(I)*
Mixed Oak-Hickory-Red Maple Forest -
Chestnut Oak-Hickory-Red Maple Forest -
Oak-Pine Forest -

Middle Elevation Zone (2500'-4500')

Classic Cove Hardwood Forest - *W ash(F)*
Acid Cove-Hemlock Forest -*W ash(I)*
Red Spruce-Northern Hardwood Forest -
Northern Hardwood Forest -*W ash(R)*
Cool Cove Forest-*W ash(I)*
Mixed Oak-Hickory-Red Maple Forest- *W ash(R)*
N. Red Oak-Hickory-Red Maple Forest -
Chestnut Oak-Hickory-Red Maple Forest -
High Elevation White Oak Forest -
Oak-Pine Forest -

High Elevation Zone (4500'-6500')

Red Spruce-Northern Hardwood Forest -
Northern Hardwood Forest -
Beech Gap Forest -
High Elev. N. Red Oak Forest -
Spruce-Fir Forest -
Fraser Fir Forest-

144

DESCRIPTION

Shade Tolerance = Intermediate
Soil Moisture Niche = Moist Sites
Vertical Preference = Dispersed Canopy

Both green and white ash have opposite compound leaves. Hickories, black walnut, mountain ash and black locust also have compound leaves, but their leaves are alternately arranged. In fact, the ashes are the only trees common in the Park with both compound and opposite leaves except yellow buckeye which displays distinctive palmately compound leaves with leaflets radiating from a central point.

Mature ash bark breaks into rectangular gray plates, but the plates are spongy. You can easily dent them with a fingernail. In winter, look for the oppositeness of the twigs; then stick a fingernail into the bark.

Distinguishing the ashes from each other is not so easy. Pull a leaf off and look at the leaf scar where the leaf attaches. Green ash leaf scars have axillary buds that stick up above the leaf scar. White ash buds are almost entirely encircled by the leaf scar. An axillary bud is the small bud found where the leaf stem attaches to the twig. Fortunately for dendro-nerds, green ash is rare in the Park, growing only occasionally along low elevation streams. White ash is the ash of the Smokies.

White ash produces winged seeds relished by wildlife. The strong resilient wood is prized for tool handles and furniture. White ash shares family connections with the olive tree, producer of edible olives without which the lowly pimento would have no proper mission in life!

IN GSMNP

White ash is a common canopy tree of the middle elevation classic cove hardwood forest. It is one of the diagnostic trees of this forest where it usually co-dominates the canopy along with yellow poplar, basswood, silverbell, red maple and occasionally hemlock.

White ash follows the stream both up and downstream from the classic cove hardwood forest where it is a dispersed canopy tree in river cove and cool cove forests. It is usually not abundant in these places, and is seldom found above 4500' elevation.

Though white ash is classed as shade intermediate, it is less tolerant than other intermediate trees. It is more abundant in pioneer (50-100 yrs.) and intermediate (100-200 yrs.) forests than in mature and climax forests.

White Basswood
(Tilia americana L. var. heterophylla)

Frequency Abbreviations:

C = Common (dominates the canopy with two or fewer associates)
F = Frequent (in the dominant canopy)
O = Occasional (frequently in dispersed canopy)
I = Infrequent (infrequent in dispersed canopy)
R=Rare

Occurrence

Low Elevation Zone (1500'-2500')

River Cove Forest *O*
Acid Cove-Hemlock Forest *I*
Mixed Oak-Hickory-Red Maple Forest *R*
Chestnut Oak-Hickory-Red Maple Forest -
Oak-Pine Forest -

Middle Elevation Zone (2500'-4500')

Classic Cove Hardwood Forest *F*
Acid Cove-Hemlock Forest *I*
Red Spruce-Northern Hardwood Forest *R*
Northern Hardwood Forest *R*
Cool Cove Forest *O*
Mixed Oak-Hickory-Red Maple Forest *R*
N. Red Oak-Hickory-Red Maple Forest *R*
Chestnut Oak-Hickory-Red Maple Forest -
High Elevation White Oak Forest -
Oak-Pine Forest -

High Elevation Zone (4500'-6500')

Red Spruce-Northern Hardwood Forest *R*
Northern Hardwood Forest *R*
Beech Gap Forest -
High Elev. N. Red Oak Forest -
Spruce-Fir Forest -
Fraser Fir Forest-

DESCRIPTION

Shade Tolerance = Tolerant
Soil Moisture Niche = Moist Sites
Vertical Preference = Canopy

Basswood has large heart-shaped leaves. So do red mulberry and Eastern redbud, but they are uncommon in the Park, occurring mainly in the low elevation zone. Basswood leaves have uneven leaf bases unlike either of the other two trees. The flower/fruit stalks of this tree arise from the surface of a long narrow leaf-shaped bract. This unusual habit immediately distinguishes basswood from all other trees. In late June, the small, round fruits of basswood literally cover the ground in places. Basswood is a very prolific sprouter, and can often be identified by numerous basal sprouts surrounding the main trunk. This is especially evident with older trees.

Basswood trees have stumped (pun intended) plant taxonomists for years in their efforts to classify its several variations into a logical body of tree names. A half-century ago, more than 16 different species were recognized in the Southeast alone. More recently, all but one (white basswood) were tossed into the taxonomic waste bin pending further study. Meanwhile basswood trees continue to grow unruffled by intellectual storms raging in the minds of men!

The straight, even grain, consistent density and light weight of basswood make it outstanding for wood carving, and it is in high demand and expensive for this reason. It's nice to know the Park's trees are forever exempted from this fate.

IN GSMNP

White basswood is a diagnostic member of the classic cove hardwood forest. It flourishes there, never growing very far from flowing water. It follows the cove upstream higher than yellow poplar and cucumbertree into the cool cove forest, but it is usually not abundant there. Basswood usually drops out by the time elevations have reached the northern hardwood forest (about 4500 feet). Unlike buckeye and yellow birch, this tree does not thrive in the frosty air of the high country.

American Beech
(*Fagus grandifolia*)

Frequency Abbreviations:
C = Common (dominates the canopy with two or fewer associates)
F = Frequent (in the dominant canopy)
O = Occasional (frequently in dispersed canopy)
I = Infrequent (infrequent in dispersed canopy)
R=Rare

Occurrence

Low Elevation Zone (1500'-2500')

River Cove Forest-*O*
Acid Cove-Hemlock Forest-*I*
Mixed Oak-Hickory-Red Maple Forest -*I*
Chestnut Oak-Hickory-Red Maple Forest -
Oak-Pine Forest -

Middle Elevation Zone (2500'-4500')

Classic Cove Hardwood Forest -*O*
Acid Cove-Hemlock Forest -*R*
Red Spruce-Northern Hardwood Forest -*F*
Northern Hardwood Forest -*F*
Cool Cove Forest-*O*
Mixed Oak-Hickory-Red Maple Forest-*I*
N. Red Oak-Hickory-Red Maple Forest -*R*
Chestnut Oak-Hickory-Red Maple Forest -
High Elevation White Oak Forest -
Oak-Pine Forest -

High Elevation Zone (4500'-6500')

Red Spruce-Northern Hardwood Forest -*F*
Northern Hardwood Forest -*F*
Beech Gap Forest -*C*
High Elev. N. Red Oak Forest -*F*
Spruce-Fir Forest -*I*
Fraser Fir Forest-

DESCRIPTION

Shade Tolerance = Tolerant
Soil Moisture Niche = Moist to Dry Sites
Vertical Preference = Canopy

American beech bark is distinctive. Even on older trees it is smooth gray. Beech leaves feel papery thin and are hairless. In autumn they turn bright yellow eventually fading to a tan color, clinging to the tree through most of the winter. Lack of wintergreen smell and taste separates American beech from the birches. The tree's long sharp-pointed buds also help. Red maple often has smooth gray bark similar to beech, but it has opposite leaves, whereas beech leaves are alternate.

American hornbeam, a diminutive beech look-a-like found in the Park has smooth gray bark, but the trunk bunches into muscle-like bulges that elicit the trees other name, musclewood. Hornbeam is always a small understory tree. Young beech trees can be in the understory, but mature beech is a canopy tree.

The beech tree is inextricably connected in history with the written word. The Anglo-Saxon word for book (bok) means beech tree, an association found in other ancient European languages. Pagan druid priests wrote sacred symbols called runes on thin tablets made from European beech wood. Eventually the runes became letters and the beech tablets became books.

IN GSMNP

Whittaker identified three separate races (white, red and gray) of American beech in GSMNP. The white race grows in the Park as an infrequent member of the dispersed canopy on moist well drained sites in the low elevation zone. It is identical to its lowland counterpart found in the Piedmont and Coastal Plain Provinces of the Southeast. The red race grows on similar sites in the middle elevation zone and is also found in the Hemlock-White Pine-Northern Hardwood Forest of the Northeastern States. The gray race grows in the high elevation zone above 4500 feet in the beech gap forest and the northern hardwood forest. It follows the Appalachian crest north to Nova Scotia.

Sadly, the beech gap forest, unique to the southern Appalachians is threatened to the point of extinction by exotic intruders. Beech bark disease, the combination of an insect and a fungus has devastated virtually every example of this community in the Park by killing the beech trees. The European wild boar which entered the Smokys around 1940 has severely damaged the herbaceous understory of beech gap forests, removing up to 30 % of the vegetation by grazing and soil rooting.

The biggest American beech trees in GSMNP measure 3 and 4 feet in diameter and 120 feet tall. As of 1996 there was a big beech on Meigs Creek Trail above the Sinks, 4 feet in diameter and 121 feet tall (Blozan 4/12/96).

Black Birch
(*Betula lenta*)

Occurrence

Low Elevation Zone (1500'-2500')

River Cove Forest *F*
Acid Cove-Hemlock Forest *F*
Mixed Oak-Hickory-Red Maple Forest *I*
Chestnut Oak-Hickory-Red Maple Forest *R*
Oak-Pine Forest -

Middle Elevation Zone (2500'-4500')

Classic Cove Hardwood Forest *O*
Acid Cove-Hemlock Forest *F*
Red Spruce-Northern Hardwood Forest *R*
Northern Hardwood Forest *I*
Cool Cove Forest *O*
Mixed Oak-Hickory-Red Maple Forest *I*
N. Red Oak-Hickory-Red Maple Forest *O*
Chestnut Oak-Hickory-Red Maple Forest *I*
High Elevation White Oak Forest -
Oak-Pine Forest -

High Elevation Zone (4500'-6500')

Red Spruce-Northern Hardwood Forest *R*
Northern Hardwood Forest *R*
Beech Gap Forest -
High Elev. N. Red Oak Forest *I*
Spruce-Fir Forest -
Fraser Fir Forest-

DESCRIPTION

Shade Tolerance = Intermediate
Vertical Preference = Canopy
Soil Moisture Niche = Moist Sites

Black birch has toothed leaves that appear to demonstrate both alternate and opposite leaf arrangement! The tree really has alternate (not opposite) leaves. Leaves on the current year's twig show this plainly, but the leaves on last year's twig sections emerge from lateral buds in pairs (two ranked), giving the appearance of opposite arrangement. Yellow birch shares this characteristic. Confusing at first, the trait actually helps separate the birches from a bunch of other trees with alternate, toothed leaves.

Young black birch bark is smooth and shiny gray with horizontal lenticels (tiny slit-like structures found on bark of several tree types). Older trees have gray-black bark often with black vertical cracks, but black birch bark never peels in thin strips like river birch or yellow birch.

Both inner bark and twigs have a delightful wintergreen taste and odor, a characteristic shared to a lesser degree by yellow birch. Black birch trees were once widely harvested to make oil of wintergreen before it was discovered the stuff could be made artificially by combining wood alcohol and salicylic acid.

Black birch is distinguished from black cherry, pin cherry and American beech by its wintergreen-flavored twigs. It's better to scratch and sniff before you taste! Black cherry and pin cherry twigs have an acrid almond-like smell when scratched. American beech bark and twigs lack lenticels and its terminal buds (buds at the twig ends) are much longer and sharper than those of black birch. Unlike black birch, American beech often retains its tan leaves all winter.

Old black birch trees are not always easily distinguished from old yellow birch trees. This might be a problem in virgin forests where old trees have thick lichen encrusted bark. Both trees are found in the cool cove forest. If you can see the twig ends look for the dark brownish color of black birch or the greenish gray color of yellow birch young twigs.

IN GSMNP

Black birch is most common in the low elevation zone in locations where moisture is abundant. In low elevation river coves it is a dominant canopy tree, and in low elevation acidic prong coves it dominates the canopy along with yellow poplar and hemlock in the acid cove-hemlock forest. Black birch follows the water courses upstream into higher country thinning out with increasing elevation. It occurs in the cool cove forest along creeks between 4000' and 4500', but it is sparse there.

Black birch also follows its preferred temperature-moisture regime by climbing the slopes with increasing elevation. It is a dominant canopy tree in the acid cove-hemlock forest on middle elevation steep protected slopes and a dispersed canopy tree in the northern red oak-hickory-red maple forest on exposed slopes. It can also be found infrequently in the dispersed canopy of the high elevation northern red oak forest of exposed ridgetops around 5000 feet elevation.

Yellow Birch
(Betula alleghaniensis)

Frequency Abbreviations:
C = Common (dominates the canopy with two or fewer associates)
F = Frequent (in the dominant canopy)
O = Occasional (frequently in dispersed canopy)
I = Infrequent (infrequent in dispersed canopy)
R=Rare

Occurrence

Low Elevation Zone (1500'-2500')

River Cove Forest-**O**
Acid Cove-Hemlock Forest-**I**
Mixed Oak-Hickory-Red Maple Forest -
Chestnut Oak-Hickory-Red Maple Forest -
Oak-Pine Forest -

Middle Elevation Zone (2500'-4500')

Classic Cove Hardwood Forest -*(I-R)*
Acid Cove-Hemlock Forest -
Red Spruce-Northern Hardwood Forest -**C**
Northern Hardwood Forest -**C**
Cool Cove Forest-**F**
Mixed Oak-Hickory-Red Maple Forest-
N. Red Oak-Hickory-Red Maple Forest -**R**
Chestnut Oak-Hickory-Red Maple Forest -
High Elevation White Oak Forest -
Oak-Pine Forest -

High Elevation Zone (4500'-6500')

Red Spruce-Northern Hardwood Forest -**C**
Northern Hardwood Forest -**C**
Beech Gap Forest -**I**
High Elev. N. Red Oak Forest -**I**
Spruce-Fir Forest -**F**
Fraser Fir Forest-**I**

155

DESCRIPTION

Shade Tolerance = Intermediate
Soil Moisture Niche = Moist Sites
Vertical Preference = Canopy

Yellow birch leaves are simple (not compound), toothed and alternate, but like black birch, the leaves on last year's twig growth appear opposite in arrangement(page 53), a trait that helps separate the birches from other toothed leaved trees.

Yellow birch is easily recognized year-round by shiny silvery-gold bark that peels into thin strips. Very old trees with lichen encrusted bark may be confused with black birch or American beech. Yellow birch twigs are grayish green while those of black birch are dark brown, but both taste of wintergreen. Yellow birch buds are short and blunt compared to the long sharply pointed buds of American beech, and unlike yellow birch, American beech often holds its papery tan leaves throughout winter.

Yellow birch embodies the image of cold moist places with crisp air and fresh breezes. Driving north on 441 toward Newfound gap on a clear autumn day, the observer is treated to golden trunks backed by the clear blue of mountain sky, ample compensation for any wilted human spirit. Whereever you are in the Park, go higher up and you will find yellow birch trees along streams and up on some of the highest peaks along with spruce and fir.

The yellow birch tree may have a reputation as a "cowboy" tree from its habit of germinating on fallen logs. Tiny yellow birch seeds can't germinate in thick leaf litter. Those lucky enough to fall on rotting logs find a suitable environment in the organic matter of decomposing logs. Often as many as one fourth of the birches in a stand have grown in this way, and when the log completely decomposes yellow birch roots remain straddling the air like a bowlegged cowboy!

IN GSMNP

Like yellow buckeye, yellow birch prefers moist cool places, but yellow birch can tolerate colder, dryer environments than yellow buckeye, and it is more abundant in terms of sheer numbers where the two trees occur together. In low elevation river coves it is occasionally found in the dispersed canopy especially as you ascend the stream, but it appears infrequently in the less favorable conditions along prong coves and in the acid cove-hemlock forest.

Along middle elevation watercourses, yellow birch is usually not abundant until the cool cove forest is encountered at about 4000 feet elevation where it becomes a dominant canopy tree flourishing in the cooler climate there.

In GSMNP yellow birch comes into its own in the high elevation forests above 4500 feet. Here it dominates the northern hardwood forest found in ravines and on exposed north-facing slopes. It also shares the canopy with red spruce on exposed ridgetops below about 6000 feet.

Like black birch, yellow birch is intermediate in shade tolerance, but it is a little more tolerant than black birch. Like most intermediate canopy trees, it will stay around to dominate the climax forest in cool moist places in the high country. There are about 26000 acres of virgin northern hardwood forest in GSMNP. Many old yellow birch trees grow protected in these forests.

Blackgum
(*Nyssa sylvatica*)

<u>Frequency Abbreviations:</u>
C = Common (dominates the canopy with two or fewer associates)
F = Frequent (in the dominant canopy)
O = Occasional (frequently in dispersed canopy)
I = Infrequent (infrequent in dispersed canopy)
R=Rare

Occurrence

Low Elevation Zone (1500'-2500')

River Cove Forest-
Acid Cove-Hemlock Forest-*I*
Mixed Oak-Hickory-Red Maple Forest -*O*
Chestnut Oak-Hickory-Red Maple Forest -*O*
Oak-Pine Forest -*O*

Middle Elevation Zone (2500'-4500')

Classic Cove Hardwood Forest-
Acid Cove-Hemlock Forest -
Red Spruce-Northern Hardwood Forest -
Northern Hardwood Forest -
Cool Cove Forest-
Mixed Oak-Hickory-Red Maple Forest-*I*
N. Red Oak-Hickory-Red Maple Forest -*I*
Chestnut Oak-Hickory-Red Maple Forest -*O*
High Elevation White Oak Forest -
Oak-Pine Forest -*O*

High Elevation Zone (4500'-6500')

Red Spruce-Northern Hardwood Forest -
Northern Hardwood Forest -
Beech Gap Forest -
High Elev. N. Red Oak Forest -
Spruce-Fir Forest -
Fraser Fir Forest-

158

DESCRIPTION

Shade Tolerance = Intermediate
Soil Moisture Niche =Moist to Dry Sites
Vertical Preference =Canopy

Blackgum leaves are teardrop-shaped. They are mostly toothless, but sometimes have a couple of large teeth near the leaf end that look like "devil horns". The leaves turn red in autumn, completing the illusion. Young blackgum twigs are consistently tan in color. The young bark resembles that of sweetgum and winged elm, neither of which is abundant in the Park. Older bark becomes decidedly blocky like dogwood. The limbs of blackgum trees emerge from the trunk at a 90 degree angle. This is a fairly distinctive characteristic.

In olden times blackgum twigs were the preferred material for tooth brushes. My grandmother, born in1903 told of dipping blackgum twigs in whiskey for tooth brushing in the days before toothpaste. Even at age 90, she had a beautiful set of teeth. She put them in a jar every night before bedtime!

IN GSMNP

In the lowlands, blackgum often haunts river margins, but up here in the mountains it is normally a tree of exposed slopes and ridgetops. Blackgum prefers the canopy, but it is always in the dispersed canopy as opposed to the dominant canopy. There is a 34-inch blackgum along the Boogerman Trail in Cataloochee in an acid cove-hemlock forest.

Black Locust
(*Robinia pseudoacacia*)

Frequency Abbreviations:
C = Common (dominates the canopy with two or fewer associates)
F = Frequent (in the dominant canopy)
O = Occasional (frequently in dispersed canopy)
I = Infrequent (infrequent in dispersed canopy)
R=Rare

Occurrence

Low Elevation Zone (1500'-2500')

River Cove Forest -
Acid Cove-Hemlock Forest -
Mixed Oak-Hickory-Red Maple Forest *I*
Chestnut Oak-Hickory-Red Maple Forest *O*
Oak-Pine Forest *I*

Middle Elevation Zone (2500'-4500')

Classic Cove Hardwood Forest -
Acid Cove-Hemlock Forest -
Red Spruce-Northern Hardwood Forest -
Northern Hardwood Forest -
Cool Cove Forest-
Mixed Oak-Hickory-Red Maple Forest *I*
N. Red Oak-Hickory-Red Maple Forest *I*
Chestnut Oak-Hickory-Red Maple Forest *O*
High Elevation White Oak Forest -
Oak-Pine Forest *R*

High Elevation Zone (4500'-6500')

Red Spruce-Northern Hardwood Forest -
Northern Hardwood Forest -
Beech Gap Forest -
High Elev. N. Red Oak Forest -
Spruce-Fir Forest -
Fraser Fir Forest-

DESCRIPTION

Shade Tolerance = Intolerant
Soil Moisture Niche = Moist-Dry Sites
Vertical Preference = Canopy

Mature black locust trees have a kind of ancient, beat-up look. The trunk usually projects upward at an angle. The bark looks blackened and uneven with thick ridges sloughing off in places, and the crown often looks thin and brown. This singular appearance can be attributed at least partially to the tree's two great natural enemies, the locust borer and the locust leaf miner. They attack their preferred host regularly, seldom killing the tree, but leaving its trunk deformed and its leaves brown. A drive through the mountains in late summer frequently reveals conspicuous groups of brown-leaved black locust trees suffering from effects of the locust leaf miner, at its peak this time of year.

Black locust has compound leaves as do hickory, ash and walnut, but unlike these trees it has thorns on the twigs. Honey locust, a scarce tree in the Park has both compound leaves and thorns, but its thorns are very long, branched (they are actually modified branches), round and wicked looking, whereas black locust thorns (actually modified stipules) look more like overgrown versions of rose thorns.

This blighted tree is a giver of good things to mankind. The beautiful creamy white flowers grace the forest in spring, and honey from them graces the table later on. Like most members of the bean family, black locust fixes nitrogen from the air, storing it in roots and branches that eventually decompose to enrich the soil. The tree's very strong rot-resistant heartwood provides the mountain farmer with outstanding posts for buildings and fences.

IN GSMNP

Three characteristics explain the distribution of black locust in the forests of GSMNP. First, it is a shade intolerant pioneer tree found most abundantly in the pioneer forest during its first 100 years of growth. Most of the Park's successional forests are entering the intermediate stage of succession at around a century in age. In these forests, black locust is fading out, with only a few large specimens scattered in the dispersed canopy. Second, black locust is about midway between yellow poplar and the yellow pines (shortleaf, Virginia, Pitch, table-mountain) in its moisture requirements. This means it is most abundant in successional forests on the slopes above the coves and below the ridge tops. Finally, black locust is mostly a low elevation tree, seldom seen above about 3500' elevation.

Yellow Buckeye
(Aesculus flava) (Aesculus octandra)

Frequency Abbreviations:
C = Common (dominates the canopy with two or fewer associates)
F = Frequent (in the dominant canopy)
O = Occasional (frequently in dispersed canopy)
I = Infrequent (infrequent in dispersed canopy)
R=Rare

Occurrence

Low Elevation Zone (1500'-2500')

River Cove Forest-*I*
Acid Cove-Hemlock Forest-*R*
Mixed Oak-Hickory-Red Maple Forest -
Chestnut Oak-Hickory-Red Maple Forest -
Oak-Pine Forest -

Middle Elevation Zone (2500'-4500')

Classic Cove Hardwood Forest -*F*
Acid Cove-Hemlock Forest -*I*
Red Spruce-Northern Hardwood Forest -*F*
Northern Hardwood Forest -*C*
Cool Cove Forest-*F*
Mixed Oak-Hickory-Red Maple Forest-
N. Red Oak-Hickory-Red Maple Forest -*R*
Chestnut Oak-Hickory-Red Maple Forest -
High Elevation White Oak Forest -*R*
Oak-Pine Forest -

High Elevation Zone (4500'-6500')

Red Spruce-Northern Hardwood Forest -*F*
Northern Hardwood Forest -*C*
Beech Gap Forest -*I*
High Elev. N. Red Oak Forest -*I*
Spruce-Fir Forest -*R*
Fraser Fir Forest-

DESCRIPTION

Shade Tolerance = Tolerant
Soil Moisture Niche = Moist Sites
Vertical Preference = Canopy

Yellow buckeye is easily identified by hand-shaped leaves with leaflets radiating from a palm-like center. The leaves are arranged in opposite pairs along the twigs. As with all opposite-leaved trees, the oppositeness carries through to the branching pattern, a useful characteristic after autumn has whisked away the leaves.

In winter, buckeye may be confused with maples and ashes since they too have opposite leaves. Look for the very stout twigs of buckeye as a clue. Mature buckeye bark breaks into thin plates that resemble jigsaw puzzle pieces. Ash bark has spongy ridges that you can dent with a fingernail. Maple bark is usually smooth gray or flaky gray.

In autumn, the tree drops dark round seeds that actually resemble the eye of a deer, hence the tree's name. It is believed the possessor of a buckeye seed receives good luck, but it is known the eater of a buckeye seed will get very sick, as they contain a dangerous chemical called glycoside. The seeds lie on the ground all winter unmolested by most wildlife and germinate in spring. They also resemble edible and delicious American chestnuts which are nearly non-existent since the chestnut blight, so be careful.

IN GSMNP

Yellow buckeye prefers cool moist places with fertile soil. It is abundant in the classic cove hardwood forest of middle elevations where it shares the canopy with a large group of trees characteristic of this rich and diverse forest. Follow the cove higher up and you find still more buckeye in the cool cove forest at the head of the cove. Here it shares dominance with yellow birch, sugar maple and perhaps red spruce on the Tennessee side of the main divide. By now yellow poplar, cucumbertree and bitternut hickory have dropped out of the mix in favor of warmer places down lower.

Yellow buckeye dominates the canopy of the high elevation northern hardwood forest with, yellow birch and American beech. It favors more moist locations here like ravines, thinning out on more exposed slopes where American beech becomes more common. Yellow buckeye is absent from the spruce-fir forest, a good diagnostic feature for distinguishing between the two forest types.

Buckeye is a shade tolerant canopy tree that remains in the climax forest. Yellow buckeyes measuring over 3 feet in diameter and 140 feet tall have been recorded in the Park.

Black Cherry (*Prunus serotina*)
Pin Cherry or Fire Cherry (*Prunus pensylvanica*)

Frequency Abbreviations:
C = Common (dominates the canopy with two or fewer associates)
F = Frequent (in the dominant canopy)
O = Occasional (frequently in dispersed canopy)
I = Infrequent (infrequent in dispersed canopy)
R=Rare

Occurrence

Low Elevation Zone (1500'-2500')

River Cove Forest-*Black C. (O)*
Acid Cove-Hemlock Forest-
Mixed Oak-Hickory-Red Maple For.- *Black C. (I)*
Chestnut Oak-Hickory-Red Maple Forest -
Oak-Pine Forest -

Middle Elevation Zone (2500'-4500')

Classic Cove Hardwood For. - *Black C. (O)*
Acid Cove-Hemlock Forest -*Black C. (I)*
Red Spruce-Northern Hardwood For. - *Black C. (I)*
Northern Hardwood Forest - *Black C. (I)*
Cool Cove Forest- *Black C. (I)*
Mixed Oak-Hickory-Red Maple For.- *Black C. (I)*
N. Red Oak-Hickory-Red Maple For.- *Black C. (R)*
Chestnut Oak-Hickory-Red Maple Forest-
High Elevation White Oak Forest -
Oak-Pine Forest -

High Elevation Zone (4500'-6500')

Red Spruce-Northern Hardwood For. - *Black C. (I)*
Northern Hardwood Forest - *Black C. (I)*
Beech Gap Forest - *Pin C. (R)*
High Elev. N. Red Oak Forest -*Pin C. (O)*
Spruce-Fir Forest -*Pin C. (O)*
Fraser Fir Forest- *Pin C. (I)*

166

DESCRIPTION

Shade Tolerance = Intolerant
Soil Moisture Niche = Moist to Dry Sites
Vertical Preference = Canopy

Cherries have simple (as opposed to compound), alternate, toothed leaves, as do beech, chestnut, sourwood and the birches. Young cherry trees have smooth shiny bark. With age, the bark breaks into irregular, dark-edged plates, but young limbs on older trees still show shiny. The shiny bark distinguishes cherries from all but the birches. Birch twigs smell and taste like wintergreen. Cherry twigs smell and taste (but don't do it!) vaguely like bitter almond. The almond smell comes from prussic acid (also called hydrocyanic acid) that contains cyanide. The cyanide poses the greatest danger in the form of dried leaves, and grazing cows have been killed after eating wilted cherry leaves.

Black knot fungus regularly attacks black cherry and pin cherry, producing distinctive black canker swellings on the trunk and branches. This is a fairly good identification characteristic when present. Black cherry and pin cherry can be distinguished from each other by bark color. Black cherry bark is silvery while pin cherry bark is shiny bronze. Black cherry leaves have a fuzzy midrib, which is lacking in fire cherry, and fire cherry leaves are much more pointed than those of black cherry. Mature fruit color is different too. Ripe black cherries are black; ripe pin cherries are red.

IN GSMNP

Both black cherry and pin cherry prefer moist, well drained sites, but pin cherry (a northern tree) replaces black cherry in the mountains above about 5000 feet elevation, with little species overlap. Black cherry is most commonly found in bottoms and along streams in the low and middle elevation zones. Pin cherry is a dependable member of the spruce-fir forest and the Fraser fir forest in the high elevation zone.

Black and pin cherries are shade intolerant pioneer trees most abundant in the developing forest (0-50 yrs.) and the pioneer forest (50-100 yrs.). Pin cherry, also called fire cherry for its tendency to form thick pioneer stands on burned-over areas, is a relatively small and short-lived tree, but black cherry remains in small numbers into the climax forest (250 + yrs.), growing quite large. There are some really big ones in the virgin forest along the Ramsey Cascades trail.

American Chestnut
(*Castanea dentata*)

Frequency Abbreviations:
C = Common (dominates the canopy with two or fewer associates)
F = Frequent (in the dominant canopy)
O = Occasional (frequently in dispersed canopy)
I = Infrequent (infrequent in dispersed canopy)
R=Rare

Occurrence

Low Elevation Zone (1500'-2500')

River Cove Forest-
Acid Cove-Hemlock Forest-**O**
Mixed Oak-Hickory-Red Maple Forest-**O**
Chestnut Oak-Hickory-Red Maple Forest -**C**
Oak-Pine Forest -

Middle Elevation Zone (2500'-4500')

Classic Cove Hardwood Forest-**I**
Acid Cove-Hemlock Forest -**I**
Red Spruce-Northern Hardwood Forest -
Northern Hardwood Forest -
Cool Cove Forest-
Mixed Oak-Hickory-Red Maple Forest-**F**
N. Red Oak-Hickory-Red Maple Forest -**C**
Chestnut Oak-Hickory-Red Maple Forest -**C**
High Elevation White Oak Forest -**F**
Oak-Pine Forest -**I**

High Elevation Zone (4500'-6500')

Red Spruce-Northern Hardwood Forest -
Northern Hardwood Forest -
Beech Gap Forest -
High Elev. N. Red Oak Forest -**F**
Spruce-Fir Forest -**O**
Fraser Fir Forest-

DESCRIPTION

Shade Tolerance =Intermediate
Soil Moisture Niche = Moist-Dry
Vertical Preference = Canopy

Obviously, the above abundance listing for American chestnut reflects the chestnut that once was, not the chestnut of today. We all fervently hope and pray this will soon change!

American chestnut leaves are long (7 inches) and narrow (2 inches) with coarse teeth. Once observed, they are not easily confused with leaves of other trees. Allegheny chinkapin, a close chestnut relative, has similar leaves, but they are usually shorter and hairy underneath as opposed to the hairless leaves of chestnut.

Presently, the American chestnut tree is an object of folklore and history. Nowhere on earth can we find American chestnut forests with trees towering 120 feet that turn the canopy a rich cream color in early summer and litter the forest floor with spiny, nut-laden burs in the fall. Victim of the exotic chestnut blight fungus, this former forest monarch was obliterated from Eastern forests by 1950. Some people and all of nature mourn its passing and await its return. The chapter (chapter 8) on exotic tree pests addresses this possibility.

IN GSMNP

Hike middle elevation exposed slopes and ridgetops. You will find the vague reflection of past glory that is today's American chestnut tree. It appears in the understory as wrist-size stump sprouts. The blight eventually finds and kills the sprouts, and if the stump has enough energy reserves, it puts up more sprouts for the blight's pleasure. The stump sprouts sometimes flower and produce fruit, but this becomes less likely with each blight cycle. We must vanquish the chestnut blight soon, because the death of each chestnut stump reduces the genetic diversity of this species. Without genetic diversity, a population lacks the ability to adapt to changes in the environment that might otherwise result in extinction.

Cucumbertree
(Magnolia acuminata)

Frequency Abbreviations:
C = Common (dominates the canopy with two or fewer associates)
F = Frequent (in the dominant canopy)
O = Occasional (frequently in dispersed canopy)
I = Infrequent (infrequent in dispersed canopy)
R=Rare
Occurrence

Low Elevation Zone (1500'-2500')

River Cove Forest *O-I*
Acid Cove-Hemlock Forest *I*
Mixed Oak-Hickory-Red Maple Forest *-R*
Chestnut Oak-Hickory-Red Maple Forest -
Oak-Pine Forest -

Middle Elevation Zone (2500'-4500')

Classic Cove Hardwood Forest *F-O*
Acid Cove-Hemlock Forest *I*
Red Spruce-Northern Hardwood Forest -
Northern Hardwood Forest -
Cool Cove Forest-
Mixed Oak-Hickory-Red Maple Forest-
N. Red Oak-Hickory-Red Maple Forest -
Chestnut Oak-Hickory-Red Maple Forest -
High Elevation White Oak Forest -
Oak-Pine Forest -

High Elevation Zone (4500'-6500')

Red Spruce-Northern Hardwood Forest -
Northern Hardwood Forest -
Beech Gap Forest -
High Elev. N. Red Oak Forest -
Spruce-Fir Forest -
Fraser Fir Forest-

DESCRIPTION

Shade Tolerance = Intolerant
Soil Moisture Niche = Moist Sites
Vertical Preference = Canopy

Cucumbertree is related by family to yellow poplar and similar in several aspects of appearance. Like yellow poplar, the bark is gray with ridges and the trunk is columnar. Both have large tulip-like flowers, but cucumbertree fruit resembles that of its closer relative, Fraser magnolia, with a red cone-shaped structure studded with bright red berry-like follicles. The name comes from the similarity of the unripe fruit to a- you guessed it- cucumber, though they are inedible. Cucumbertree leaves are elliptical in shape instead of lobed like those of yellow poplar, and like all magnolia family members the twigs are encircled by stipular rings, distinctive rings surrounding the twig at the leaf base. Unlike Fraser magnolia, cucumbertree leaves lack ear-shaped leaf bases.

Cucumbertree has light-weight easily worked wood like yellow poplar. It was harvested along with yellow poplar, white pine and hemlock during the early days of logging when splash dams were used to float logs down stream. The low density, light weight logs of these species were much easier to float downstream than the heavier oaks and hickories.

An interesting naturally-occurring variety of the cucumbertree with canary yellow flowers grows only in a few locations in Georgia. It is called yellow cucumber-tree (*Magnolia acuminata var. cordata*). This rare tree was first described in the wild by the botanist Michaux in the mid 1800's, but was not rediscovered in the wild until 1913. Today it is cultivated and sold in nurseries as an ornamental tree.

IN GSMNP
Cucumbertree is abundant in the Park only in the classic cove hardwood forest of middle elevations. It is generally far less numerous here than yellow poplar, but in some places like Cucumber Gap near Elkmont it dominates along with poplar and mountain silverbell in a majestic example of the classic cove hardwood forest.

Cucumbertree is a shade intolerant pioneer tree like yellow poplar, though it is slightly more tolerant. Like yellow poplar it grows rapidly, but it is not long lived like poplar, surviving only about 150 years in the forest. It is far less abundant than yellow poplar because birds and rodents eat the seeds, and its seedlings succumb more readily to frost and drought. There is a 3.5 foot diameter cucumbertree, 145 feet tall along Baxter Creek in the Cataloochee District.

Fraser Fir
(Abies fraseri)

Frequency Abbreviations:
C = Common (dominates the canopy with two or fewer associates)
F = Frequent (in the dominant canopy)
O = Occasional (frequently in dispersed canopy)
I = Infrequent (infrequent in dispersed canopy)
R=Rare

Occurrence

Low Elevation Zone (1500'-2500')

River Cove Forest
Acid Cove-Hemlock Forest
Mixed Oak-Hickory-Red Maple Forest -
Chestnut Oak-Hickory-Red Maple Forest -
Oak-Pine Forest -

Middle Elevation Zone (2500'-4500')

Classic Cove Hardwood Forest -
Acid Cove-Hemlock Forest -
Red Spruce-Northern Hardwood Forest -
Northern Hardwood Forest -
Cool Cove Forest-
Mixed Oak-Hickory-Red Maple Forest-
N. Red Oak-Hickory-Red Maple Forest -
Chestnut Oak-Hickory-Red Maple Forest -
High Elevation White Oak Forest -
Oak-Pine Forest -

High Elevation Zone (4500'-6500')

Red Spruce-Northern Hardwood Forest -*I*
Northern Hardwood Forest -*I*
Beech Gap Forest -*I*
High Elev. N. Red Oak Forest -*R*
Spruce-Fir Forest -*F*
Fraser Fir Forest-*C*

DESCRIPTION

Shade Tolerance = Tolerant
Soil Moisture Niche = Moist Sites
Vertical Preference = Canopy

Fraser fir needles are soft, flat and arranged in horizontal rows on the twigs. Eastern hemlock needles share these characteristics, but have silvery stripes on the needle undersides, and the two trees are rarely found growing together. Red spruce needles are stiff and angle-sided with sharp points.

Unfortunately, most old-growth Fraser fir trees are now easily recognized by bare lifeless trunks, work of the balsam wooly adelgid. Look for living trees as seedlings growing thickly below the dead trunks. The adelgid doesn't attack until the tree is old enough to produce rough bark. This takes about 20 years, and at that age, the tree also begins producing seeds. Hopefully this means the tree may be able to survive in its native habitat until some effective treatment can be found to restore it.

Though greatly threatened in the wild, Fraser fir is alive and well as America's most popular Christmas tree. Fraser fir is grown on Christmas tree farms by the millions. North Carolina alone produces more than 5 million Fraser fir Christmas trees annually. The tree ranks number 1 in needle retention and softness, and is considered outstanding for its beautiful color and fragrant aroma.

John Fraser, a Scottish botanist first discovered and described Fraser fir in 1787 while on a botanizing foray into the Southern mountains with famous French botanist Andre Michaux. Legend has it that Fraser annoyed Michaux who thought he talked too much. One night the horses wandered off, and as a pretext to rid himself of the loud mouthed botanist, Michaux suggested he would find the horses while Fraser pushed on along the trail. As a result, Fraser found the firs first. Perhaps Michaux considered murder at this point! If so, he refrained and we have both Fraser fir and Fraser magnolia which, incidentally, was actually first described by William Bartram; another story.

.

Excellent Fraser fir habitat is found on all topographic positions above 6000 feet elevation. These high cold places experience fog more than 240 days a year. The fog provides significant water in the form of condensation, a phenomena similar to that of the coast redwoods of California which are frequently bathed in fogs wafted in from the Pacific Ocean.

Below 6000 feet Fraser fir mixes with red spruce in the spruce-fir forest found on exposed slopes and ridgetops between 5000 and 6000 feet. These stands are now strongly dominated by Red Spruce alone with a dense understory of fir seedlings along with a variety of other trees and shrubs.

Eastern Hemlock
(*Tsuga canadensis*)

Frequency Abbreviations:
C = Common (dominates the canopy with two or fewer associates)
F = Frequent (in the dominant canopy)
O = Occasional (frequently in dispersed canopy)
I = Infrequent (infrequent in dispersed canopy)
R=Rare

Occurrence

Low Elevation Zone (1500'-2500')
River Cove Forest *F*
Acid Cove-Hemlock Forest-*C*
    (diagnostic of this forest type)
Mixed Oak-Hickory-Red Maple Forest -*I*
Chestnut Oak-Hickory-Red Maple Forest -
Oak-Pine Forest -

Middle Elevation Zone (2500'-4500')

Classic Cove Hardwood Forest -*C-F*
Acid Cove-Hemlock Forest -*C*
Red Spruce-Northern Hardwood Forest -*I*
Northern Hardwood Forest -*I*
Cool Cove Forest-*I*
Mixed Oak-Hickory-Red Maple Forest-*I*
N. Red Oak-Hickory-Red Maple Forest -*R*
Chestnut Oak-Hickory-Red Maple Forest -
High Elevation White Oak Forest -
Oak-Pine Forest -

High Elevation Zone (4500'-6500')

Red Spruce-Northern Hardwood Forest -*I*
Northern Hardwood Forest -*I*
Beech Gap Forest -
High Elev. N. Red Oak Forest -*R*
Spruce-Fir Forest -*R*
Fraser Fir Forest-

DESCRIPTION

Shade Tolerance = Very Tolerant
Soil Moisture Niche = Moist Acidic Sites
Vertical Preference = Canopy

Evergreen boughs and pine-like bark make this conifer easy to identify. Large hemlocks with high foliage can sometimes be confused with white pine. Look on the ground beneath the tree. Hemlock needles are short, flat and blunt-tipped. White pine needles are long, needle-like and come in bundles of five. At higher elevations, where they occasionally occur together, hemlock and red spruce may be confused. Hemlock needles are short, flat and blunt-tipped. Red spruce needles are round or angle-sided and sharp pointed. Hemlock and Fraser fir rarely coincide, but just in case; Fraser fir twigs are tan colored with globe-shaped resinous terminal buds. Scratch Fraser fir twigs; you will smell Christmas! Hemlock twigs are dark colored without obvious terminal buds.

Eastern hemlock is a tree of poetry and legend, or so Longfellow thought when he wrote of the forest primeval in <u>Evangeline</u>. Huge trunks rising one hundred and fifty feet above a bubbling prong supporting a mantle of evergreen boughs sparkling in summer sunlight, create an impression of wild power and beauty well deserving of poetic expression. A century ago, visitors to these mountains routinely slept on beds of fragrant hemlock boughs, a practice today's environmentally conscious campers no longer subscribe to. It is also against Park regulations!

The Park harbors at least 3000 acres of virgin hemlock forest. Sadly, the hemlock wooly adelgid is rapidly decimating these magnificent trees. For more information on the battle to save the hemlocks, the reader is referred to chapter 8 on exotic tree pests.

In GSMNP

Hemlock thrives in deep shade and on acidic soils. Though indifferent to soil nutrients, it must not venture far from the water of streams or the ample soil moisture found on cool moist protected slopes.

In low elevation river cove forests it shares the canopy with a variety of trees including American sycamore, the diagnostic tree for this forest type.

In mid-succession (intermediate stage) acid cove-hemlock forests, it shares the canopy with poplar, red maple and black birch. As the acid cove-hemlock forest matures, hemlock assumes exclusive dominance by virtue of its extreme shade tolerance and longevity. Rosebay rhododendron often forms the understory in these forests, giving them what Whittaker called, "a somber aspect unrelieved by the verdant green of the deciduous forest." Hemlocks can live on in the climax forest for centuries. Trees exceeding 500 years in age have been documented in Eastern North America, including GSMNP.

Hemlock often shares the canopy with a large mix of trees including white basswood, mountain silverbell, yellow poplar, yellow buckeye, white ash and sugar maple in the classic cove hardwood forest of middle elevations, and it follows the streams up into the cool cove forest on the North Carolina side, where it grows more sparingly with yellow birch, yellow buckeye and basswood. On upper slopes around 4500 feet elevation hemlock mingles with red spruce and the northern hardwood forest.

The Park has been renowned for giant hemlocks, but the story is almost too sad to tell. The tallest recorded Eastern Hemlock on earth planet was the Usis hemlock located in the Cataloochee District. At 173.1 feet Usis was the tallest of a select group of hemlocks exceeding 170 feet in height. Usis is dead now and only one of the select group, the Noland Mountain Hemlock, survives as of July, 2009. At 171.5 feet tall and 4 feet 4 inches dbh it is the tallest known living Eastern hemlock. The largest hemlock (by wood volume) ever recorded also lived in the Cataloochee District and is also dead.

Both trees were located along Caldwell Creek in Cataloochee where one of the oldest and most magnificent hemlock forests in existence once flourished. Thanks to Will Blozen and the Eastern Native Tree Society we have documented information on these incredible trees, alive now only in Blozen's photographs and memory.

Hickory

Bitternut Hickory *(Carya cordiformis)*
Mockernut Hickory *(Carya alba or Carya tomentosa)*
Pignut Hickory *(Carya glabra)*

Frequency Abbreviations:
C = Common (dominates the canopy with two or fewer associates)
F = Frequent (in the dominant canopy)
O = Occasional (frequently in dispersed canopy)
I = Infrequent (infrequent in dispersed canopy)
R=Rare

Occurrence

Low Elevation Zone (1500'-2500')

River Cove Forest- ***Bitternut (I)***
Acid Cove-Hemlock Forest
Mixed Oak-Hickory-Red Maple Forest..- ***Pig.(F),***
Mock.(O)
Chestnut Oak-Hickory-Red Maple Forest - ***Pig.(F),***
Mock. (R)

Oak-Pine Forest -

Middle Elevation Zone (2500'-4500')

Classic Cove Hardwood Forest -***Bitternut (O)***
Acid Cove-Hemlock Forest -
Red Spruce-Northern Hardwood Forest -
Northern Hardwood Forest -
Cool Cove Forest-
Mixed Oak-Hickory-Red Maple Forest- ***Pig. (F)***
N. Red Oak-Hickory-Red Maple Forest - ***Pig. (F)***
Chestnut Oak-Hickory-Red Maple Forest - ***Pig. (F)***
High Elevation White Oak Forest -
Oak-Pine Forest -

High Elevation Zone (4500'-6500')

Red Spruce-Northern Hardwood Forest -
Northern Hardwood Forest -
Beech Gap Forest -
High Elev. N. Red Oak Forest -
Spruce-Fir Forest -
Fraser Fir Forest-

DESCRIPTION

Shade Tolerance = Tolerant
Soil Moisture Niche = Dry Sites
Vertical Preference = Canopy

The hickories are a confusing bunch of trees even to botanists, because the different kinds readily cross with each other creating hybrids that are hard to identify down to the species level. They are fairly distinctive as a group, however, because they have compound leaves. Compound leaves are leaves with multiple leaflets. Pecan and walnut are two widely known examples. Determining just what is and isn't a leaf can be confusing. Theoretically, a small bud (axillary bud) arises where the leaf stem emerges from the twig. If you find this bud, you know you are looking at a leaf. This axillary bud may not be visible, so you need more clues to help. Frequently, as with ash trees, the leaf base is swollen where it attaches to the twig. Notice also that leaflets are attached to a non-woody greenish leaf stem, whereas leaves are attached to at least a partially woody twig.

For the memory-impaired dendrologist an acronym exists for recalling the main trees with compound leaves (**HAL** **P**eeking over the **W**all). It stands for **H**ickory, **A**sh, **L**ocusts, **P**ecan, **W**alnut. "Locusts" is plural implying black locust and honeylocust, both with compound leaves. American yellowwood, another tree with compound leaves found sparingly in the Park, is not covered by the acronym. Yellowwood, a beautiful member of the bean family, is increasingly used as an ornamental plant.

IN GSMNP

Pignut hickory is probably the most common hickory in the Park. Of its fellow hickories, it likes the driest sites like exposed slopes, but it is also common on protected slopes. The vast majority of pignut leaves have 5 leaflets. The nuts are pear-shaped with a tapered end that could resemble a pig's nose. The black nut husks usually do not split open after dropping.

Mockernut hickory is another common hickory in the Park. It prefers sites that are not too dry, like protected slopes and protected ridgetops. Mockernut hickory leaves come with 7 to 9 leaflets per leaf, but almost never with 5 leaflets. The nuts are big, round and enclosed by a thick black husk that splits open after dropping to reveal the extremely hard tan nut shell. Mockernut twigs are stout, thicker than any other hickory. The twigs and leaflets are hairy and have a strong aroma when crushed.

American Indians figured out how to utilize hickory nuts without laboriously cracking them to extract the rich meat. They put the nuts (minus the black husk) into their mortars and pounded them with wooden pestles, shell and all into a meal. The meal went into a pot of water (probably heated) where the tiny pieces of shell sank to the bottom and a sweet creamy liquid, rich in oil, was poured off the top and saved. They called this liquid "pawcohiccora" which means hickory milk, mixing it with cornmeal to make nutritious and delicious cakes.

Unlike its fellow hickories, bitternut hickory, also common in the Park grows in moist rich cove forests, being most common in the classic cove hardwood forest of middle elevations. Its presence there constitutes the easiest way to distinguish it from its fellow hickories. The buds too are distinctive, composed of just 2 sulfur-yellow bud scales that attach to each other like a long narrow clam shell. Dendrologists use the term valvate to describe this condition. Bitternut has 7-11 leaflets per leaf. The bark often appears grayish or whitish in patches, constituting another fairly common distinguishing feature.

Fraser Magnolia
(Magnolia fraseri)

Frequency Abbreviations:
C = Common (dominates the canopy with two or fewer associates)
F = Frequent (in the dominant canopy)
O = Occasional (frequently in dispersed canopy)
I = Infrequent (infrequent in dispersed canopy)
R=Rare

Occurrence

Low Elevation Zone (1500'-2500')

River Cove Forest-*I*
Acid Cove-Hemlock Forest-*O*
Mixed Oak-Hickory-Red Maple Forest -*O*
Chestnut Oak-Hickory-Red Maple Forest -*O*
Oak-Pine Forest -

Middle Elevation Zone (2500'-4500')

Classic Cove Hardwood Forest-*I*
Acid Cove-Hemlock Forest -*O*
Red Spruce-Northern Hardwood Forest -
Northern Hardwood Forest -
Cool Cove Forest-*R*
Mixed Oak-Hickory-Red Maple Forest-*O*
N. Red Oak-Hickory-Red Maple Forest -*O*
Chestnut Oak-Hickory-Red Maple Forest -*I*
High Elevation White Oak Forest -
Oak-Pine Forest -

High Elevation Zone (4500'-6500')

Red Spruce-Northern Hardwood Forest -
Northern Hardwood Forest -
Beech Gap Forest -
High Elev. N. Red Oak Forest -*R*
Spruce-Fir Forest -
Fraser Fir Forest-

DESCRIPTION

Shade Tolerance =Intermediate
Soil Moisture Niche =Moist-Dry, Acidic Sites
Vertical Preference =Canopy and Subcanopy

Three species of deciduous magnolias grow in GSMNP. All three prefer moist well drained sites near streams. Cucumbertree (*Magnolia acuminata*) becomes a large canopy tree, sharing many characteristics with yellow poplar (*Liriodendron tulipifera*), another member of the magnolia family but not of the genus *Magnolia*. Fraser magnolia (*Magnolia fraseri*) can become a canopy tree, but is found as often in the subcanopy. Its leaves are long and narrow with distinctive "ear lobes" at the base. Umbrella magnolia (*Magnolia tripetala*) is usually an understory tree. Its leaves lack ears.

Fraser and umbrella magnolias are easily identified when leaves are present, because their leaves are large (12 inches or more in length). Look also for the one to two-inch long purple terminal buds on the twig ends, and the stipular rings encircling the twigs that mark all members of the magnolia family. The leaf ears distinguish Fraser from umbrella. In winter, look for the multiple trunks of Fraser magnolia, a prolific sprouter, and check the ground for shed leaves.

IN GSMNP

Fraser magnolia is most commonly found along creeks and lower protected slopes in the middle elevation zone in the acid cove-hemlock forest, and on protected and exposed slopes in several oak-hickory-red maple forests. It is never abundant in these forests, comprising less than 10 percent of the trees. There is a Fraser magnolia on the upper reaches of Deep Creek with a 22-inch diameter stem that is part of a multi-stemmed tree.

Red Maple
(Acer rubrum)

Frequency Abbreviations:
C = Common (dominates the canopy with two or fewer associates)
F = Frequent (in the dominant canopy)
O = Occasional (frequently in dispersed canopy)
I = Infrequent (infrequent in dispersed canopy)
R=Rare

Occurrence

Low Elevation Zone (1500'-2500')

River Cove Forest-*I*
Acid Cove-Hemlock Forest-*O*
Mixed Oak-Hickory-Red Maple Forest -*F*
Chestnut Oak-Hickory-Red Maple Forest -*F*
Oak-Pine Forest -*I*

Middle Elevation Zone (2500'-4500')

Classic Cove Hardwood Forest -*O*
Acid Cove-Hemlock Forest -*O*
Red Spruce-Northern Hardwood Forest -
Northern Hardwood Forest -
Cool Cove Forest-*I*
Mixed Oak-Hickory-Red Maple Forest-*F*
N. Red Oak-Hickory-Red Maple Forest -*F*
Chestnut Oak-Hickory-Red Maple Forest -*F*
High Elevation White Oak Forest -*I*
Oak-Pine Forest -*I*

High Elevation Zone (4500'-6500')

Red Spruce-Northern Hardwood Forest -*R*
Northern Hardwood Forest -*R*
Beech Gap Forest -
High Elev. N. Red Oak Forest -*I*
Spruce-Fir Forest -
Fraser Fir Forest-

DESCRIPTION

Shade Tolerance = Intermediate
Soil Moisture Niche = Moist to Dry Sites
Vertical Preference = Canopy

Red maple has opposite leaves. This separates it from a bunch of other trees with alternate leaves. Among maples, its leaves have teeth on the lobes, in contrast to sugar maple which has toothless lobes just like its image on the Canadian flag. Some part of the red maple tree is red year round. In summer the leaf stems are red. In fall the leaves often turn red. Winter twigs are red, and in spring the flowers and seeds are bright red. Sugar maple flowers are yellow and its seeds are greenish or rusty, but not bright red. Look for red maple flowers in very early spring (Feb.-March) in contrast to those of sugar maple which appear in late spring (April-May).

Red maple is the most widespread tree in the eastern U. S. It flourishes from Miami to Halifax and west to the Mississippi River with the exception of most of Illinois. It is true to its nature in GSMNP where it occurs in all three elevation zones up to about 5500 feet, outstripping other maples in abundance on most sites. It usually loses out to sugar maple on the richest cove sites and to mountain maple on the highest elevation sites.

Red maple's reputation for exceptional adaptability is due to a genetic condition called polyploidy shared by many members of the plant community. What is polyploidy? Most people have 2 sets of chromosomes, one from each parent. Visualize beads on a string. Each string is a chromosome, and each bead is a gene. You get one set of chromosomes (one string) from your dad (23 chromosomes) and one set from your mom (23 more chromosomes). Combined in you, the two sets of chromosomes determine your genetic makeup.

Polyploid individuals somehow get more than one set of dad chromosomes and more than one mom set. These duplicate chromosome sets give an organism powerful adaptive abilities. Combine the polyploid state of red maple with the great variation in elevation and landform presented by the southern Appalachians, and you get a bunch of red maple races or ecotypes ready to fill just about any niche. Though red maple is the king of multiple chromosomes, other mountain trees such as American beech, northern red oak, white oak and basswood also exhibit this trait to a lesser degree.

IN GSMNP
Red maple is most abundant as a canopy tree in the various oak-hickory-red maple forests found on low and middle elevation slopes. It has been an important replacement tree in these forests for the blight-killed American chestnut tree. This makes sense. As a shade intermediate tree, red maple specializes in waiting in the understory for an opening to rapidly fill. Its polyploidy induced adaptability has given it robust survivability on former chestnut sites, so it was ready and able to fill the gaps when the chestnut trees died. It is edged out in this role on dryer exposed slopes where chestnut oak has become the most important chestnut replacement.

Sugar Maple
(Acer saccharum)

Frequency Abbreviations:
C = Common (dominates the canopy with two or fewer associates)
F = Frequent (in the dominant canopy)
O = Occasional (frequently in dispersed canopy)
I = Infrequent (infrequent in dispersed canopy)
R=Rare

Occurrence

Low Elevation Zone (1500'-2500')

River Cove Forest-*O*
Acid Cove-Hemlock Forest-*I*
Mixed Oak-Hickory-Red Maple Forest -*I*
Chestnut Oak-Hickory-Red Maple Forest -*R*
Oak-Pine Forest -

Middle Elevation Zone (2500'-4500')

Classic Cove Hardwood Forest -*F*
Acid Cove-Hemlock Forest -*I*
Red Spruce-Northern Hardwood Forest -
Northern Hardwood Forest -*O*
Cool Cove Forest-*F*
Mixed Oak-Hickory-Red Maple Forest-
N. Red Oak-Hickory-Red Maple Forest -*R*
Chestnut Oak-Hickory-Red Maple Forest -*R*
High Elevation White Oak Forest -
Oak-Pine Forest -

High Elevation Zone (4500'-6500')

Red Spruce-Northern Hardwood Forest -**O**
Northern Hardwood Forest -*O*
Beech Gap Forest -*I*
High Elev. N. Red Oak Forest -*I*
Spruce-Fir Forest -*I*
Fraser Fir Forest-

DESCRIPTION

Shade Tolerance = Very Tolerant
Soil Moisture Niche = Moist Sites
Vertical Preference = Canopy

Sugar maple leaves look like the Canadian flag... or vice versa. Like all maples, the leaves are arranged in pairs opposite each other on the twigs. This fulfills the letter M in the acronym MAD DOGS, a useful tool for remembering trees with opposite leaves:

Maple
Ash
Dogwood

Somehow buckeye and catalpa got left out of the acronym. Perhaps we should re-render it as MADogs and Buckeyed Cats!

Sugar maple is distinguished from other maples in the Park by the lack of teeth on its leaf lobes. Chalk maple and Southern sugar maple also have toothless lobes, but they are absent from the Park. Red maple has toothed lobes, and is present and far more common at all elevations than sugar maple. Silver maple has very toothed lobes, but it is fairly uncommon. Striped maple and mountain maple are always small trees in the understory, and their leaf shapes have little to do with the Canadian flag!

Sugar maple is one of the most valuable trees in eastern America. Maple syrup comes from its sap. One gallon of syrup requires 30 gallons of sugar maple sap. Classified by woodworkers as a hard maple, its wood is denser than that of other maples and considered outstanding for construction of fine furniture and flooring. The autumn glory of sugar maple is legendary, providing a display of color unsurpassed in the tree world.

IN GSMNP

Sugar maple loves moist nutrient-rich soil and is abundant where this occurs. It is most common in middle elevation coves (classic cove hardwood forest) in situations where the soil has excellent moisture-holding qualities and is rich in nutrients. Here it is a dominant canopy tree. It is also a dominant canopy tree in the cool cove forest at the head of coves where rich soil prevails. In other cove forests it is more or less abundant as a dispersed canopy tree.

Sugar maple is very shade tolerant and long lived. We would expect to see it in the mature climax forest on moist rich sites after a century or more of forest succession.

Chestnut Oak
(Quercus prinus)

Frequency Abbreviations:
C = Common (dominates the canopy with two or fewer associates)
F = Frequent (in the dominant canopy)
O = Occasional (frequently in dispersed canopy)
I = Infrequent (infrequent in dispersed canopy)
R=Rare

Occurrence

Low Elevation Zone (1500'-2500')

River Cove Forest (diagnostic of this forest type) **-**
Acid Cove-Hemlock Forest -
Mixed Oak-Hickory-Red Maple Forest *F*
Chestnut Oak-Hickory-Red Maple Forest *C*
Oak-Pine Forest *F*

Middle Elevation Zone (2500'-4500')

Classic Cove Hardwood Forest -
Acid Cove-Hemlock Forest -
Red Spruce-Northern Hardwood Forest -
Northern Hardwood Forest -
Cool Cove Forest-
Mixed Oak-Hickory-Red Maple Forest *F*
N. Red Oak-Hickory-Red Maple Forest *O*
Chestnut Oak-Hickory-Red Maple Forest *C*
High Elevation White Oak Forest *I*
Oak-Pine Forest *O*

High Elevation Zone (4500'-6500')

Red Spruce-Northern Hardwood Forest -
Northern Hardwood Forest -
Beech Gap Forest -
High Elev. N. Red Oak Forest -
Spruce-Fir Forest -
Fraser Fir Forest-

DESCRIPTION

Shade Tolerance = Intermediate
Soil Moisture Niche = Dry Sites
Vertical Preference = Canopy

Chestnut oak is a member of the white oak group of oaks characterized by rounded leaf lobes, usually lacking bristles on the lobe tips, grayish (instead of blackish) bark and acorns that mature in one growing season. Chestnut oak leaves are easily recognized by the wavy, scalloped leaf edges. The bark on mature trees is also distinctive with its deep furrows and broad flat topped ridges.

Probably named for the resemblance of its leaves to those of American chestnut, the chestnut oak produces the largest acorns in the eastern U. S. Like other members of the white oak group, they are low in a bitter preservative called tannin, and wildlife prefer them over those of the tannin-rich red oak group. They often drop in autumn before those of other oaks, providing excellent early mast for wildlife.

Chestnut oak once grew side-by-side with American chestnut trees in former American chestnut forests on exposed slopes and exposed ridgetops. With the chestnut's demise, chestnut oak has become the replacement tree, but despite their size, its acorns provide a poor substitute for American chestnuts that once carpeted the forest floor.

GSMNP

In the low elevation zone, chestnut oak is a common component of the mixed oak-hickory-red maple forest, especially on dryer sites. In both low and middle elevation zones it is the dominant tree on exposed slopes where it often shares the canopy with scarlet oak, pignut hickory and red maple.

On acidic sites, the understory of the chestnut oak forest is often completely dominated by Heath family members. On dry acidic sites, mountain laurel is the dominant Heath. On more moist acidic sites, rhododendron fills this niche. These forests, called chestnut oak-heath forests, frequently form a band between the acid cove-hemlock forest on lower protected slopes and ridgetop chestnut oak-hickory-red maple forests.

.

Northern Red Oak
(Quercus rubra)

Frequency Abbreviations:
C = Common (dominates the canopy with two or fewer associates)
F = Frequent (in the dominant canopy)
O = Occasional (frequently in dispersed canopy)
I = Infrequent (infrequent in dispersed canopy)
R=Rare

Occurrence

Low Elevation Zone (1500'-2500')

River Cove Forest-*I*
Acid Cove-Hemlock Forest-*I*
Mixed Oak-Hickory-Red Maple Forest -*F*
Chestnut Oak-Hickory-Red Maple Forest -*F*
Oak-Pine Forest -*I*

Middle Elevation Zone (2500'-4500')

Classic Cove Hardwood Forest -*R-I*
Acid Cove-Hemlock Forest -*I*
Red Spruce-Northern Hardwood Forest -
Northern Hardwood Forest -
Cool Cove Forest-*R*
Mixed Oak-Hickory-Red Maple Forest-*F*
N. Red Oak-Hickory-Red Maple Forest -*C*
Chestnut Oak-Hickory-Red Maple Forest -*F*
High Elevation White Oak Forest -*O*
Oak-Pine Forest -*I*

High Elevation Zone (4500'-6500')

Red Spruce-Northern Hardwood Forest -*R*
Northern Hardwood Forest -*I*
Beech Gap Forest -*R*
High Elev. N. Red Oak Forest -*C*
Spruce-Fir Forest -
Fraser Fir Forest-

DESCRIPTION

Shade Tolerance = Intermediate
Soil Moisture Niche = Cool, Moist-Dry Sites
Vertical Preference = Canopy

Everything about this tree is big. Northern red oak usually has big, bear paw-shaped leaves that look similar to those of black oak but are hairless below. Black oak leaves are fuzzy underneath, especially along the veins. The acorns of northern red oak are big and barrel shaped, nearly as wide as long, and the usually big trunk has wide flat gray stripes running much of its length. Scarlet oak is similar in general appearance, but has smaller leaves with deep indentions (sinuses) between the lobes. Its acorns aren't as big as those of northern red oak and usually have concentric rings scribed around the acorn tip. Scarlet also has the gray stripes, but they are narrower and much less defined than those of northern red oak, and scarlet oak, a poor self-pruner, usually has dead limbs clinging to its trunk, a characteristic northern red oak lacks.

Whittaker felt this tree exhibited two genetic races or strains in the Park. The lowland race found in middle and low elevation zones also ranges far south into the Piedmont and Coastal Plain provinces. The high elevation race which he called 'borealis' is found in the high elevation zone, where it is adapted to the cold climate found there. Physically, the two races may have slightly different leaf shapes, with the borealis race exhibiting longer leaves with deeper lobes. The presence of tree races is similar to the existence of many dog breeds. Each breed exhibits special adaptations to its environment, but all are able to interbreed and are thus considered a single species. The idea of tree races developing in areas with large environmental gradients is logical, and Whittaker noted many trees in the southern Appalachians that exhibited two or more adaptive races.

IN GSMNP

Northern red oak is the king of oaks in the southern Appalachians. It dominates its name-sake forests on exposed ridgetops at 5000 feet in the high elevation zone, accompanied by yellow birch and occasionally red spruce. It also dominates the northern red oak-hickory-red maple forest on middle elevation exposed slopes. In addition, it is found in the canopy of nearly all other oak forest types, and infrequently in the oak-pine forest.

Northern red oak likes cool places. With this criterion met it can stand drought and nutrient-poor soil. It cannot compete with yellow birch and buckeye on cool moist sites, and it cannot reach much above 5000 feet into the realm of the red spruce.

Northern red oak is intermediate in shade tolerance, but it is more shade tolerant than all other oaks except white oak. It becomes a member of the climax forest and can live on there for centuries.

In 1996 Will Blozan measured a northern red oak on the west bank of Boulevard Prong that towered 139 .1 feet and was 5 feet 6 inches in diameter.

Scarlet Oak
(Quercus coccinea)

Frequency Abbreviations:
C = Common (dominates the canopy with two or fewer associates)
F = Frequent (in the dominant canopy)
O = Occasional (frequently in dispersed canopy)
I = Infrequent (infrequent in dispersed canopy)
R=Rare

Occurrence

Low Elevation Zone (1500'-2500')

River Cove Forest-
Acid Cove-Hemlock Forest
Mixed Oak-Hickory-Red Maple Forest -*O*
Chestnut Oak-Hickory-Red Maple Forest -*F*
Oak-Pine Forest -*C*

Middle Elevation Zone (2500'-4500')

Classic Cove Hardwood Forest -
Acid Cove-Hemlock Forest -
Red Spruce-Northern Hardwood Forest -
Northern Hardwood Forest -
Cool Cove Forest-
Mixed Oak-Hickory-Red Maple Forest-*O*
N. Red Oak-Hickory-Red Maple Forest -*I*
Chestnut Oak-Hickory-Red Maple Forest -*F*
High Elevation White Oak Forest -
Oak-Pine Forest -*F*

High Elevation Zone (4500'-6500')

Red Spruce-Northern Hardwood Forest -
Northern Hardwood Forest -
Beech Gap Forest -
High Elev. N. Red Oak Forest -
Spruce-Fir Forest -
Fraser Fir Forest-

197

DESCRIPTION

Shade Tolerance = Intermediate
Soil Moisture Niche = Dry Sites
Vertical Preference = Canopy

A member of the red oak group, scarlet oak has leaves with pointed, bristle-tipped lobes characteristic of this group of oaks which includes northern red, black, southern red and shingle oak. In contrast to the big bear paw leaves of northern red and black oak, scarlet oak's leaf lobes are quite narrow with deep indentions (called sinuses) between them. To a bunch of bucolic forest dendrology students (98 % male), the shapely leaves and common name of this tree gave rise to visions of Gone With The Wind and, yes, Scarlet O'Hara. The analogies between this tree and the antebellum heroine go deeper than can be safely related here, but it worked. We seldom failed to identify this tree correctly on field quizzes!

A poor self-pruner, scarlet oak often retains dead limbs on its lower trunk, a characteristic separating it from northern red oak, which usually has a clean, trunk, free of dead limbs.

Scarlet oak leaves do turn scarlet in autumn. In good color years this creates a stunning effect on mountain slopes, highlighting these trees among their peers. The acorns are easily identified too. Scarlet oak acorn caps are reddish and flaky and the acorn tip is nearly always surrounded by a broken indented ring.

IN GSMNP

Scarlet oak is a dry site oak most abundant on low and middle elevation exposed slopes and ridgetops, where it is usually accompanied by pines. In years past, these sites were often dominated nearly exclusively by pines like Virginia, shortleaf and pitch pine, as they are the pioneer species on dry sites. As forest succession proceeds on these sites, albeit at a slow pace, dry site oaks like scarlet and black oak become more prominent.
Scarlet oak regularly mixes with northern red, white and chestnut oaks on middle elevation slopes, but it does not dominate these sites.

White Oak
(Quercus alba)

Frequency Abbreviations:
C = Common (dominates the canopy with two or fewer associates)
F = Frequent (in the dominant canopy)
O = Occasional (frequently in dispersed canopy)
I = Infrequent (infrequent in dispersed canopy)
R=Rare

Occurrence

Low Elevation Zone (1500'-2500')

River Cove Forest-
Acid Cove-Hemlock Forest-*I*
Mixed Oak-Hickory-Red Maple Forest -*F*
Chestnut Oak-Hickory-Red Maple Forest -*O*
Oak-Pine Forest -*I*

Middle Elevation Zone (2500'-4500')

Classic Cove Hardwood Forest -
Acid Cove-Hemlock Forest -
Red Spruce-Northern Hardwood Forest -
Northern Hardwood Forest -
Cool Cove Forest-
Mixed Oak-Hickory-Red Maple Forest-*O*
N. Red Oak-Hickory-Red Maple Forest -*I*
Chestnut Oak-Hickory-Red Maple Forest -*I*
High Elevation White Oak Forest -*C*
Oak-Pine Forest -*I*

High Elevation Zone (4500'-6500')

Red Spruce-Northern Hardwood Forest -
Northern Hardwood Forest -
Beech Gap Forest -
High Elev. N. Red Oak Forest -
Spruce-Fir Forest -
Fraser Fir Forest-

DESCRIPTION

Shade Tolerance = Intermediate
Soil Moisture Niche = Moist-Dry Sites
Vertical Preference = Canopy

Namesake of the white oak group, this tree's leaves exhibit the blunt lobes without bristle tips that help define this group of oaks, including post oak, and chestnut oak in the Park. Mature white oak bark breaks into beautiful and distinctive light gray flaky strips easily recognized in the forest. White oak acorns are bullet shaped instead of barrel shaped like those of northern red oak or giant-size like those of chestnut oak. They lack both the concentric rings around the tip and flaky acorn cap of scarlet oak.

The mountain farmer saw the white oak tree as an indispensable resource. His hogs fattened on its acorns. The deer, turkey, squirrel and bear he hunted also subsisted on its mast. His bones were warmed by long-burning white oak logs crackling in the fireplace on frosty winter nights. He split a 4-foot diameter white oak section into hundreds of shingles for his cabin roof. His cabin itself was made of chestnut or yellow poplar, but nearly everything inside was made of white oak. He split an 8- inch white oak sapling into quarters to make furniture, and split the quarters down further into white oak splits for making chair bottoms and baskets. He dosed himself with a medicinal tea made from the tannin-rich bark. And yes, there were times when he just stopped and stared at beautiful white oaks glowing amber on a fine autumn day. We can appreciate this tree's majestic beauty as well as its role as a bridge between the world of nature and the world of man.

IN GSMNP

White oak is abundant in the low elevation mixed oak-hickory-red maple forest. It prefers the well drained middle slopes, leaving the lower north-facing slopes to northern red oak and the dryer higher slopes to chestnut and scarlet oak, but there is much overlap and mixing of oaks in these low elevation forests.

In the middle elevation zone, white oak is the dominant tree in the high elevation white oak forest found on exposed ridgetops between 4000 and 4500 feet elevation. Here it once shared the canopy with American chestnut. Now only chestnut stump sprouts survive. South of the range of red spruce, northern red oak and white oak form stunted forests that dominate most exposed ridgetops, with northern red oak occupying the richer cooler sites and white oak on the dryer warmer sites.

The Ramsey Cascades Trail is home to a 123-foot tall white oak 4 feet in diameter.

Eastern White Pine
(Pinus strobus)

<u>Frequency Abbreviations:</u>
C = Common (dominates the canopy with two or fewer associates)
F = Frequent (in the dominant canopy)
O = Occasional (frequently in dispersed canopy)
I = Infrequent (infrequent in dispersed canopy)
R=Rare

Occurrence

Low Elevation Zone (1500'-2500')

River Cove Forest-*I*
Acid Cove-Hemlock Forest-(*F-O*)
Mixed Oak-Hickory-Red Maple Forest -*O*
Chestnut Oak-Hickory-Red Maple Forest -*O*
Oak-Pine Forest -*(F-O)*

Middle Elevation Zone (2500'-4500')

Classic Cove Hardwood Forest -
Acid Cove-Hemlock Forest -*I*
Red Spruce-Northern Hardwood Forest -
Northern Hardwood Forest -
Cool Cove Forest-
Mixed Oak-Hickory-Red Maple Forest-
N. Red Oak-Hickory-Red Maple Forest -
Chestnut Oak-Hickory-Red Maple Forest -*I*
High Elevation White Oak Forest -
Oak-Pine Forest -*R*

High Elevation Zone (4500'-6500')

Red Spruce-Northern Hardwood Forest -
Northern Hardwood Forest -
Beech Gap Forest -
High Elev. N. Red Oak Forest -
Spruce-Fir Forest -
Fraser Fir Forest-

DESCRIPTION

Shade Tolerance = Intermediate
Soil Moisture Niche = Moist-Dry Sites
Vertical Preference = Canopy

All pines have needles arranged in bundles held together by a short bundle sheath. White pine is easily distinguished from other pines (yellow pines) by its 5-needles-per-bundle arrangement. Virginia, shortleaf and table mountain pines have 2 needles per bundle, and pitch pine has 3 needles per bundle. White pine's branches extend from the trunk bunched together in whorls, a trait yellow pines do not share. The cones of this tree look quite different from those of the yellow pines. They are less prickly and usually dotted with small white resin globs. They smell like Christmas.

White pine is famed as the tree of choice for masts during the great age of sailing ships. Agents of the British navy often located prime mast trees, marking them with the king's broad arrow symbol signifying hands off to everyone else. The city of Kingstree, South Carolina is said to be named for a lone white pine growing far south of its natural range marked by the king's men and destined for the royal navy.

IN GSMNP

White pine is a tree of the Park's low elevation zone (1500-2500'). It is most abundant on slopes and ridgetops both protected and exposed. Here it grows with dry site oaks like chestnut oak and scarlet oak and with other pines. White pine is less commonly found growing with hemlock on creek flats and along prongs and rivers as an infrequent dispersed canopy tree.

Like other pines, white pine can act as a pioneer tree where it forms the dominant canopy during the pioneer stage of forest succession. This usually happens on old fields or burned over areas where competition from hardwood trees is minimal, but it is classified as intermediate in shade tolerance and more often behaves like an oak or maple taking advantage of sunny gaps in the canopy to gain dominance. Unlike other pines, white pine is long lived and survives well into the climax forest.

This tree is fairly abundant in some areas of the Park and scarce in others. Along the Abrams Creek watershed in the Cades Cove district it teams up with hemlock sharing dominance in forests that appear to be fairly old based on size of the trees. It is common in the forests of the Cataloochee district, where it grows to great height and girth. The Boogerman white Pine there grew 207 feet tall before being topped by a tornado. At 188.5 feet it is still the tallest accurately measured tree of any kind east of the Rocky Mountains.

White pine is less abundant along Oconaluftee River, West Prong Pigeon River and Little River than along the streams described above. These areas were heavily logged, and white pine is a very desirable lumber tree. Also, there is less low elevation land along these streams than along those mentioned above.

Yellow Pines

Shortleaf Pine (*Pinus echinata***)**
Pitch Pine (*Pinus rigida*)
Table-mountain Pine (*Pinus pungens*)
Virginia Pine (*Pinus virginiana*)
Frequency Abbreviations:
C = Common (dominates the canopy with two or fewer associates)
F = Frequent (in the dominant canopy)
O = Occasional (frequently in dispersed canopy)
I = Infrequent (infrequent in dispersed canopy)
R=Rare

Occurrence

Low Elevation Zone (1500'-2500')

River Cove Forest-
Acid Cove-Hemlock Forest
Mixed Oak-Hickory-Red Maple For. - *Va. Pine (I)*
Sht. Pine (I)

Chestnut Oak-Hickory-Red Maple F.*Va. Pine (O)*
Sht. Pine (I)

Oak-Pine Forest - *Va. Pine (F), Sht. Pine (F-O)*

Middle Elevation Zone (2500'-4500')

Classic Cove Hardwood Forest -
Acid Cove-Hemlock Forest -
Red Spruce-Northern Hardwood Forest -
Northern Hardwood Forest -
Cool Cove Forest-
Mixed Oak-Hickory-Red Maple F..- *Pitch Pine (I)*
N. Red Oak-Hickory-Red Maple Forest -
Chestnut Oak-Hickory-Red Maple F.- *Pitch Pine*
(I)

High Elevation White Oak Forest -
Oak-Pine Forest --*Pitch Pine (F), TM Pine (O)*

High Elevation Zone (4500'-6500')

> Red Spruce-Northern Hardwood Forest -
> Northern Hardwood Forest -
> Beech Gap Forest -
> High Elev. N. Red Oak Forest -
> Spruce-Fir Forest -
> Fraser Fir Forest-

DESCRIPTION

Shade Tolerance = Intolerant
   Soil Moisture Niche = Very Dry Sites
   Vertical Preference = Canopy

The term yellow pine is logger's language referring to a group of similar southern pines whose wood produces lumber that is relatively dense, yellow in color and contains significant quantities of extractable resin. The group includes shortleaf, Virginia, pitch, table-mountain, loblolly, slash, longleaf and pond pines.

Yellow pines are distinguished from white pine by having fewer than 5 needles per bundle. The wood of yellow pines is denser and yellow in color compared to that of white pine. Virginia pine has 2 needles per bundle, reddish bark and frequently retains its dead lower limbs, giving it a scraggly appearance. It is primarily a tree of the low elevation zone (1500-2500'). Shortleaf, also a low elevation zone pine, has 2 needles per bundle, but lacks the reddish bark and scraggly appearance of Virginia pine. Shortleaf bark is unique among pines in bearing pitch pockets, pencil lead-size holes containing resin. Pitch pine has 3 needles per bundle and is primarily a tree of the middle elevation zone (2500-4500'). Table-mountain pine has 2 needles per bundle, but it is fairly scarce in the Park, occurring mostly between 3500 and 4500 feet in elevation-far above the habitat of Virginia pine.

IN GSMNP

In the past, fires started by lightening and by man burned dry rocky exposed slopes and ridgetops clean. Subsequently, yellow pines seeded in to exclusively dominate these sites. The wholesale logging operations of the early 1900's left huge piles of tree tops which burned, creating more bare land where yellow pine forests sprang up.

As these early succession pine forests age, the yellow pines will continue to drop out in favor of dry site oaks, like scarlet and chestnut oaks, that dominate later stages of succession.

The Park Service has traditionally suppressed fires that would generate more pine forests, but table-mountain pine, a tree found only in Appalachia, requires the heat of a forest fire to open its cones for seed dispersal. The Park Service is now making special efforts to burn portions of its habitat to stimulate seed production to preserve this unique tree in the Park.

Yellow Poplar
(Liriodendron tulipifera)

<u>Frequency Abbreviations:</u>
C = Common (dominates the canopy with two or fewer associates)
F = Frequent (in the dominant canopy)
O = Occasional (frequently in dispersed canopy)
I = Infrequent (infrequent in dispersed canopy)
R=Rare

Occurrence

Low Elevation Zone (1500'-2500')

River Cove Forest-*F*
Acid Cove-Hemlock Forest-*F*
Mixed Oak-Hickory-Red Maple Forest -*O*
Chestnut Oak-Hickory-Red Maple Forest -*O*
Oak-Pine Forest -

Middle Elevation Zone (2500'-4500')

Classic Cove Hardwood Forest -*F*
Acid Cove-Hemlock Forest -*O*
Red Spruce-Northern Hardwood Forest -
Northern Hardwood Forest -
Cool Cove Forest-*R*
Mixed Oak-Hickory-Red Maple Forest-*I*
N. Red Oak-Hickory-Red Maple Forest -*O*
Chestnut Oak-Hickory-Red Maple Forest -*I*
High Elevation White Oak Forest -
Oak-Pine Forest -

High Elevation Zone (4500'-6500')

Red Spruce-Northern Hardwood Forest -
Northern Hardwood Forest -
Beech Gap Forest -
High Elev. N. Red Oak Forest -
Spruce-Fir Forest -
Fraser Fir Forest-

DESCRIPTION

Shade Tolerance = Intolerant
Soil Moisture Niche = Moist, well drained Sites
Vertical Preference = Canopy

Yellow poplar leaves have a distinctive shape easily recognized by most people. They resemble a tulip in outline, but it is the large tulip-like yellow flowers that inspired the alternate name of tuliptree. Also distinctive is the tree's columnar trunk, rising to a height of 150 feet or more. American Indians made dugout canoes from these mighty trunks of soft light-weight wood, easily worked with stone tools in conjunction with fire.

An often unsuspected member of the magnolia family, yellow poplar shares several traits with its showier but less majestic relatives. All have showy flowers, and all wear rings, stipular rings that is. Stipules are circular scars, borne on the twig where the leaves arise. Magnolia family members display stipules as distinctive rings surrounding the twig at the leaf base. This unique characteristic is useful during sessions of winter botany, the dendrological nemesis of the aspiring tree nerd!

Yellow poplar is one of the first trees to unfold leaves in spring and one of the first to release them in autumn. They always turn some shade between light yellow and orange, creating a striking appearance against a deep blue autumn sky.

IN GSMNP

This tree loves sunny, moist, well drained sites, but it does not tolerate cold, dropping out of GSMNP forests between 4000 and 4500 feet elevation. Yellow poplar is abundant and dominant in low elevation coves where it often dominates the canopy with American sycamore, black birch, red maple and hemlock. It is found to a lesser degree on all other low elevation landforms except exposed ridgetops, where it is excluded by the dry, nutrient-poor environment.

Yellow poplar is also abundant and dominant in the classic cove hardwood forest of middle elevations, but there it shares dominance with a larger group of trees. Follow the stream up to the cool cove forest, and you will find this tree drops out in favor of yellow buckeye and yellow birch.

A shade intolerant pioneer tree, yellow poplar is more abundant on all sites it occupies during the pioneer (50-100 yrs.) and intermediate (100-200 yrs.) stages of forest succession. In mature (200-250 yrs.) and climax (250 + yrs.) forests it is much less abundant, but often the oldest and largest tree encountered.

Thousands of acres of land in the Park began growing new forests between 75 and 100 years ago as farming and logging ceased prior to the Park's designation. These forests are now transitioning from pioneer forests containing lots of intolerant pioneer trees like yellow poplar and black locust to intermediate forests where intermediates and shade tolerant trees dominate. Now, yellow poplar is abundant in these forests on moist, well drained locations. Another century of forest succession will see its numbers greatly decline, while the few survivors will live on in the climax forest as great old giants.

The Park is famous for its ancient giant yellow poplars. One along the Ramsey Cascades trail is 7 feet in diameter. The Albright Grove of big yellow poplars in the Cosby District has several trees in the 6 to 8 feet diameter range. The world champion yellow poplar is called the Sag Branch poplar located in the Boogerman Grove, Cataloochee District. At 167 feet tall and 10.4 feet diameter, it reigns supreme in a race of giants.

Mountain Silverbell
(Halesia tetraptera var. monticola)

Frequency Abbreviations:

C = Common (dominates the canopy with two or fewer associates)
F = Frequent (in the dominant canopy)
O = Occasional (frequently in dispersed canopy)
I = Infrequent (infrequent in dispersed canopy)
R=Rare

Occurrence

Low Elevation Zone (1500'-2500')

River Cove Forest-(*F-O*)
Acid Cove-Hemlock Forest-*I*
Mixed Oak-Hickory-Red Maple Forest -*R*
Chestnut Oak-Hickory-Red Maple Forest -
Oak-Pine Forest -

Middle Elevation Zone (2500'-4500')

Classic Cove Hardwood Forest -*F*
Acid Cove-Hemlock Forest -*O*
Red Spruce-Northern Hardwood Forest -
Northern Hardwood Forest -
Cool Cove Forest-*R*
Mixed Oak-Hickory-Red Maple Forest-*R*
N. Red Oak-Hickory-Red Maple Forest -*I*
Chestnut Oak-Hickory-Red Maple Forest -
High Elevation White Oak Forest -
Oak-Pine Forest -

High Elevation Zone (4500'-6500')

Red Spruce-Northern Hardwood Forest -*I*
Northern Hardwood Forest -*I*
Beech Gap Forest -*O*
High Elev. N. Red Oak Forest -*I*
Spruce-Fir Forest -*R*
Fraser Fir Forest-

DESCRIPTION

Shade Tolerance = Tolerant
Soil Moisture Niche = Moist Sites
Vertical Preference = Canopy

Mountain silverbell has alternate (not opposite) simple (not compound) toothed leaves as do many other Park trees including serviceberry, mountain holly, cherries, birches and sourwood. The tree's bark, however separates it from its fellows. Young silverbell bark has distinctive stripes like those of striped maple. Don't worry. You can't confuse the two trees, because striped maple has opposite, lobed leaves like all other maples. Older silverbell bark breaks into distinctive reddish flakes that are readily recognized. The beautiful white flowers of this tree are also distinctive and have given us two common names. Mountain folks called it peawood in reference to its pea-like flowers. The bell shaped petal arrangement evokes the more popular name of silverbell.

In fact, this tree has so many names, confusion has arisen as a result. In the old days of plant taxonomy, botanists called the tree mountain silverbell and gave it the Latin name, *Halesia monticola*. More recently, the tree has been reclassified as a variety of the more widespread Carolina silverbell, *Halesia carolina*. Scientists now call it *Halesia tetraptera var. monticola*, but <u>humans</u> still call it mountain silverbell or peawood! Just kidding, scientists. We love you!

IN GSMNP

Silverbell grows along streams in the low and middle elevation zones. It makes regular appearances in the river cove forest, and can be abundant in the classic cove hardwood forest. By about 3500 feet elevation, silverbell has shifted with its preferred habitat on to protected slopes where it graces the acid cove-hemlock forest. In the high elevation zone (4500-6500+) feet, silverbell moves on to exposed slopes and exposed ridgetops as a member of the northern hardwood forest and the high elevation northern red oak forest. It is also fairly abundant in some beech gap forests.

Red Spruce
(Picea rubens)

Frequency Abbreviations:
C = Common (dominates the canopy with two or fewer associates)
F = Frequent (in the dominant canopy)
O = Occasional (frequently in dispersed canopy)
I = Infrequent (infrequent in dispersed canopy)
R=Rare

Occurrence

Low Elevation Zone (1500'-2500')

River Cove Forest
Acid Cove-Hemlock Forest
Mixed Oak-Hickory-Red Maple Forest -
Chestnut Oak-Hickory-Red Maple Forest -
Oak-Pine Forest -

Middle Elevation Zone (2500'-4500')

Classic Cove Hardwood Forest -
Acid Cove-Hemlock Forest *-R*
Red Spruce-Northern Hardwood Forest -
Northern Hardwood Forest *-R*
Cool Cove Forest-*R*
Mixed Oak-Hickory-Red Maple Forest-
N. Red Oak-Hickory-Red Maple Forest -
Chestnut Oak-Hickory-Red Maple Forest -
High Elevation White Oak Forest -
Oak-Pine Forest -

High Elevation Zone (4500'-6500')

Red Spruce-Northern Hardwood Forest *-F*
Northern Hardwood Forest *-I*
Beech Gap Forest *-R*
High Elev. N. Red Oak Forest *-I*
Spruce-Fir Forest *-C*
Fraser Fir Forest-*C*

213

DESCRIPTION

Shade Tolerance = Very Tolerant
Soil Moisture Niche = Dry-Moist Sites
Vertical Preference = Canopy

Red spruce is easily distinguished from pines by most folks. It can only be confused in the Park with Fraser fir and Eastern hemlock. Spruce needles are stiff, angle-sided and have sharp pointed ends. They are arranged all around the twig. Both fir and hemlock needles are soft, flattened and arranged in horizontal rows along the twig. Spruce cones always project down on the twig. Fir cones always project up on the twigs. It took me years to find a mnemonic to help with remembering this fact. The names spruce ('spruce up') and fir (fir can stick up or down) don't help! Finally I found it. The words fir and air both have 3 letters and end in 'ir'. Fir cones always stick into the air!

No better wood exists for acoustic guitar tops than red spruce. The resonating qualities of the wood are outstanding and improve with age of both the tree and the instrument. The wood's very high strength-to-weight ratio accounts for its excellence. These same characteristics found it as an important structural component in the flying Jennies of the First World War.

Traditional mountain remedies often contained oils and resins called balsam made from the sap of coniferous trees, so these trees came to be called balsam trees. Fraser fir has white resin blisters in the bark that reminded people of milk, so they named Fraser fir she-balsam. They called red spruce he-balsam and made remedies for sore throats, cuts, boils and other ailments from the sap of both trees.

IN GSMNP

Red spruce clothes the high country seldom dipping below 4000 feet elevation. The southern extent of its geographic range occurs in the Park at about Siler's Bald with no red spruce growing southwest of this point.

Red spruce dominates the spruce-fir forests found on all landforms between 5000 and 6000 feet elevation. Most of the Fraser fir in these forests occurs as seedlings in the wake of the balsam wooly adelgid. Yellow birch and pin cherry are fairly common, with some hemlock mixing in on warmer lower sites. Mountain maple and mountain ash thrive in the understory.

Between 4000 feet and 5000 feet in ravines and on north slopes on the cool Tennessee side, red spruce mixes with the northern hardwoods in the red spruce-northern hardwood forest where it is a dominant canopy tree. Yellow birch, yellow buckeye and American beech are its associates here.

Red spruce thins out above 6000 feet elevation giving way to Fraser fir, the most cold hardy of southern Appalachians conifers.

American Sycamore
(Platanus occidentalis)

Frequency Abbreviations:
C = Common (dominates the canopy with two or fewer associates)
F = Frequent (in the dominant canopy)
O = Occasional (frequently in dispersed canopy)
I = Infrequent (infrequent in dispersed canopy)
R=Rare
Occurrence

Low Elevation Zone (1500'-2500')

River Cove Forest (diagnostic of this forest type) *F*
Acid Cove-Hemlock Forest *I*
Mixed Oak-Hickory-Red Maple Forest -
Chestnut Oak-Hickory-Red Maple Forest -
Oak-Pine Forest -

Middle Elevation Zone (2500'-4500')

Classic Cove Hardwood Forest -
Acid Cove-Hemlock Forest -
Red Spruce-Northern Hardwood Forest -
Northern Hardwood Forest -
Cool Cove Forest-
Mixed Oak-Hickory-Red Maple Forest-
N. Red Oak-Hickory-Red Maple Forest -
Chestnut Oak-Hickory-Red Maple Forest -
White Oak-Hickory-Red Maple Forest -
High Elevation White Oak Forest -
Oak-Pine Forest -

High Elevation Zone (4500'-6500')

Red Spruce-Northern Hardwood Forest -
Northern Hardwood Forest -
Beech Gap Forest -
High Elev. N. Red Oak Forest -
Spruce-Fir Forest -
Fraser Fir Forest-

DESCRIPTION

Shade Tolerance = Intermediate
Soil Moisture Niche = Moist Sites along streams
Vertical Preference = Canopy

American sycamore is one of the easiest trees to identify. Its stark white upper trunk contrasts strikingly with its associates. Lower on the trunk the tan bark peels off in flaky strips or plates. The broad shallowly lobed leaves might be confused with those of maple, but they are arranged alternately on the twig, whereas maple leaves are arranged in opposite pairs.

This tree loves water, so never plant one near your septic tank! On good moist sites along streams, sycamore can grow to be huge. Specimens have been found in the Mississippi valley with trunks 15 feet in diameter reaching 180 feet in height.

Most large sycamores are hollow, making excellent dens for animals and good hiding places for our pioneer ancestors. According to his biographer, in 1770, Daniel Boone and his brother-in-law John Stuart were hunting in Kentucky when Stuart failed to return one evening. Five years later Boone found his remains and powder horn inside a large hollow sycamore tree where he had apparently hidden, presumably after being wounded by Indians. This tale may be tall or short, but it shore makes a good story!

IN GSMNP

A tree of low elevation rivers and prongs, sycamore is diagnostic of the low elevation river cove forest where it is rarely dominant but almost always present as a member of the dispersed canopy.

Sycamore is specifically adapted to stream environments. It becomes established on the site in the wake of streamside pioneer trees like black willow and hazel alder. Though intermediate in shade tolerance, it is only slightly more shade tolerant than the pioneers. The open space provided by the stream corridor lets in enough sunlight to meet its needs, and we often see sycamores leaning well out into the stream channel to catch the light.

A long-lived tree, sycamore remains into the climax forest along with a few yellow poplars and shade tolerant trees like basswood, sugar maple and hemlock.

TREE PAGES

Dogwoods
Alternate-leaf Dogwood *(Cornus alternifolia)*
Flowering Dogwood *(Cornus florida)*

DESCRIPTION

Shade Tolerance =Very Tolerant
Soil Moisture Niche =Moist-Dry
Vertical Preference =Understory

Flowering dogwood has opposite, toothless leaves with leaf veins running roughly parallel to each other. The flowers are renowned for their springtime beauty. Each one is actually a central bunch of small nondescript greenish flowers surrounded by four large white structures that look like flower petals but are actually flower bracts. Only botanists care about the difference! The tree produces bright red berries that are technically really drupes, another botany term. Flowering dogwood bark breaks into distinctive small square plates nearly black in color. Some folks call it alligator bark.

Flowering dogwood is a low elevation zone tree, where it is fairly widespread from stream sides to exposed slopes and ridgetops. Dogwood anthracnose *(Discula destructiva)*, an exotic fungus has killed many flowering dogwood trees in GSMNP. Oddly, the disease does not bother alternate-leaf dogwood.

Alternate-leaf dogwood has, you guessed it, alternate leaves. This makes it unique in the American dogwood genus. Its most distinguishing characteristic is the greenish color of the twigs. The young bark is usually smooth and greenish too. Alternate-leaf dogwood flowers are white but not big and showy. The fruit is dark blue.

Alternate-leaf dogwood is not nearly as common in the Park as flowering dogwood. It grows mostly in the northern hardwood forest and the red spruce-northern hardwood forest, not venturing in abundance much below 4000 feet elevation, except occasionally along streams.

Hobblebush
(Viburnum lantanoides)

DESCRIPTION

Shade Tolerance =Tolerant
Soil Moisture Niche =Moist Sites
Vertical Preference =Understory

Hobblebush is a small understory shrub. It has opposite heart-shaped leaves that might be mistaken for basswood, except basswood has alternate leaves. Hobblebush, also called witch hobble, produces bright orange-red berries, while basswood has a unique looking, but not near as showy, nut-like fruit. Their elevational ranges do not overlap either. That helps.

Hobblebush and both striped and mountain maples share habitats and have opposite leaves, but the maples have lobed leaves, while hobblebush leaves are unlobed.

IN GSMNP

Hobblebush is a diagnostic shrub of the spruce-fir forest. It is also common in the northern hardwood forest, red spruce-northern hardwood forest and the Fraser fir forest. This little cold-hardy shrub does not venture below 4500 feet elevation.

American Holly
(Ilex opaca)

DESCRIPTION

Shade Tolerance =Tolerant
Soil Moisture Niche =Moist-Dry, Acidic Sites
Vertical Preference =Subcanopy

American holly is one of the easiest trees to recognize. It is
evergreen, has thick spine-tipped "holly" leaves and smooth white
or grayish bark. This tree seems to occur either as solitary
individuals or thickly with no in-between. Perhaps the birds that
relish its red berries have something to do with this?

American holly and its close relative mountain holly share the
genus name, Ilex. Both like acidic sites and produce bright red
holly berries. The similarities end there, however. American holly
is evergreen. It is a tree of the low elevation zone, whereas
mountain holly is deciduous and loves the high elevation zone.

IN GSMNP

In the Park, American holly is most likely to occur in the acid
cove-hemlock forest and the mixed oak-hickory-red maple forest
of the low elevation zone (1500-2500'). It is found to some extent
in the river cove forest too.

Mountain Holly
(Ilex montana)

DESCRIPTION

Shade Tolerance =Tolerant
Soil Moisture Niche =Moist-Dry, Acidic Sites
Vertical Preference =Understory

Mountain holly has alternate, deciduous, oval shaped toothed leaves. The leaves have sunken veins. That is, the veins appear sunken slightly below the leaf surface. This gives them a kind of wrinkled appearance. The leaves are borne on short spur branches. This sometimes gives them a whorled appearance. Mountain holly bark is grayish and nondescript. The red holly berry fruit often stays on the tree all winter long

Allegheny serviceberry is the most likely tree to mistake for mountain holly. Serviceberry leaves don't have sunken veins, but they do often have heart-shaped bases. Serviceberry bark has dark vertical slits that mountain holly bark lacks.

IN GSMNP

A shade tolerant understory tree, mountain holly seldom exceeds 30 feet in height. It is most abundant in the high elevation zone, where it inhabits all forest types except the beech gap forest and the Fraser fir forest. In the middle elevation zone, mountain holly is often found in the northern red oak-hickory-red maple forest.

American Hornbeam
(Carpinus caroliniana)

DESCRIPTION

Shade Tolerance =Tolerant
Soil Moisture Niche =Moist Sites
Vertical Preference =Understory

This tree is also called musclewood due to the muscular bulges on its usually small trunk. Ironwood is another of its names, referring to the dense iron-like hardness of its wood, second in hardness only to dogwood. It is also called blue beech because it has smooth gray bark like beech, though usually darker in color. The muscles help distinguish hornbeam from beech.

Hornbeam leaves are simple and toothed like beech leaves, but they look entirely different. They are smaller and are hairy on the underside. Beech leaves have a papery feel that hornbeam leaves lack.

Hornbeam is a member of the birch family, and its leaves resemble those of black birch and yellow birch, but it lacks the shiny, peeling bark of the birches.

IN GSMNP

American hornbeam is diagnostic of the river cove forest, where it grows in the understory below sycamore and other river cove trees. It rarely ventures above the low elevation zone (1500-2500'), and always grows along streams.

Umbrella Magnolia
(Magnolia tripetala)

DESCRIPTION

Shade Tolerance =Tolerant
Soil Moisture Niche =Moist Sites
Vertical Preference =Understory

This tree is unmistakable in the forest. The leaves are 20 inches long and 10 inches wide and broadly elliptical in shape. They lack the characteristic "ear lobed" base displayed by Fraser magnolia leaves. Umbrella magnolia leaves emerge from the twigs in spiral clusters that simulate an open umbrella, the tree's namesake. Leafless, the tree resembles its sib Fraser magnolia. Search the ground for cast-off leaves to distinguish between them. If it's a big tree in the subcanopy or canopy, it is most likely to be Fraser magnolia, as umbrella rarely exceeds understory height.

IN GSMNP

Umbrella magnolia is a low elevation understory tree in the Park. It grows mainly along streams and low protected slopes where it sometimes mixes in with Fraser magnolia, its more abundant sib. Unlike Fraser magnolia, however, umbrella magnolia does not climb the slopes or venture far above 2500 feet elevation.

Understory Maples
Mountain maple *(Acer spicatum)*
Striped maple *(Acer pennsylvanicum)*

DESCRIPTION

Shade Tolerance =Tolerant
Soil Moisture Niche =Moist-Dry, Acidic Sites
Vertical Preference =Understory

Like all other maples, striped and mountain maples have opposite leaves with lobes. Striped maple leaves have three distinct lobes that make them look like goose feet. In fact, many folks call the tree goose foot maple. The leaf lobes have fine teeth. Mountain maple leaves have three to five lobes and the lobes have very coarse teeth. Young striped maple bark is striped, hence the name. Mountain maple bark is stripeless. Striped maple flower/fruit stalks always point down, while mountain maple flower/fruit stalks always point up, toward the high mountains, preferred habitat of this tree.

Striped maple is usually taller than mountain maple, venturing into the subcanopy on favorable sites. Mountain maple is as often shrub size as it is tree size.

Mountain maple might be confused with young red maples. This will only be a problem in the high elevation zone where the two trees overlap. Young mountain maple twigs are slightly fuzzy while those of red maple lack fuzz.

Striped maple is more widespread in the Park than mountain maple. It is most abundant in the middle elevation zone along streams, especially in the classic cove hardwood forest, but it also ventures on to protected slopes. Here it is found in the mixed oak-hickory-red maple forest and the northern red oak-hickory-red maple forest. Striped maple becomes sparse above 5000 feet.

On the other hand, mountain maple loves the high elevation zone, occurring most abundantly in the red spruce-northern hardwood forest, the spruce-fir forest and the Fraser fir forest.

Mountain Ash
(Sorbus americana)

DESCRIPTION

Shade Tolerance =Tolerant
Soil Moisture Niche =Moist Sites
Vertical Preference =Subcanopy

Mountain ash (also called American mountain ash) has alternate compound leaves. Found only in the Spruce-fir forest, the Fraser fir forest and occasionally the beech gap forest, no other tree in these forest types has compound leaves.

Mountain ash is completely unrelated to the other two trees that bear its common name, white ash and green ash. Its compound leaves are alternate instead of opposite like the two ashes, and it bears bright orange berry-like pomes instead of the winged seeds of the two ashes. In the southern Appalachians, mountain ash never grows below 5000 feet. White ash and green ash never grow above 5000 feet. Of course, never say never, so let's just say 99 and 44 one hundredths percent pure never!

In Europe, trees of the genus Sorbus are called Rowan trees, and they figure greatly in European folklore. The European rowan tree (*S. aucuparia*) is fabled in England as the tree upon which the devil hanged his mother! Our mountain ash bears no such folkish stigma. It is a beautiful colorful tree whose bright red berries are relished by birds and bears.

IN GSMNP

Mountain ash is a subcanopy tree in the spruce-fir forest and the Fraser fir forest, and it is a diagnostic species in these forests just as sycamore is diagnostic of the river cove forest. The mountain ash sawfly, a native pest, often defoliates this tree, but rarely kills it.

Mountain Laurel
(Kalmia latifolia)

DESCRIPTION

Shade Tolerance =Tolerant
Soil Moisture Niche =Dry, Acidic Sites
Vertical Preference =Understory

Mountain laurel is a thicket-forming evergreen shrub with leathery elliptical leaves that shine in the sun. The shrub's zig-zag stems often give it a twisted look. It resembles rosebay rhododendron slightly, but its leaves are much smaller, and the shrub itself is usually smaller in size than rosebay.

The green leaves of mountain laurel are toxic to cows, deer, goats and sheep, but not to dogs and cats. Who figured this out, and how?

Mountain laurel flowers are quite lovely. Small bowl-shaped blossoms marked on the inside with purple spots in a radial pattern, they grow in white to pinkish clusters that weigh down the boughs in good years. Demonstrating nature's finesse, the flowers combine beauty and functionality to create a very effective pollinating device. The pollen-bearing stamens are "cocked" back into recesses marked by the tiny purple spots. When a bee lands on the flower and brushes the stamens, they fire off, slapping him in the face, and dosing his fuzzy body with pollen for transport to the next flower!

IN GSMNP

Mountain laurel is abundant in the Park. Like rhododendron, it is a member of the acid-loving Heath (Ericaceae) family, is thicket-forming, and often dominates the understory of forests where it occurs. It differs from rhododendron in its affinity for dry, nutrient-poor slopes and ridgetops. Mountain laurel is a common understory shrub on exposed slopes and ridgetops in the low and middle elevation zones. These landforms are the realm of the mixed oak-hickory-red maple forest, the chestnut oak-hickory-red maple forest, the northern red oak-hickory-red maple forest and the high elevation white oak forest. Its highest occurrence is around 5000 feet elevation, where it is found in the high elevation northern red oak forest and on heath balds.

On protected slopes and ridgetops, mountain laurel shares the understory with rhododendron. Mountain laurel usually takes the hotter, dryer south-facing slopes while rhodo is more common on cooler north-facing slopes.

Mountain laurel is usually far less abundant in coves and flats than rhododendron. Presumably, rhodo is able to out-compete laurel on these sites.

Rosebay Rhododendron
(*Rhododendron maximum*)

DESCRIPTION

Shade Tolerance =Tolerant
Soil Moisture Niche =Moist Sites
Vertical Preference =Understory

Rhododendron is an evergreen understory shrub that grows to about 30 feet. It is very abundant in GSMNP and most folks recognize the thick evergreen leaves that measure about 8 inches in length. Rhododendron leaves curl up conspicuously in cold weather, a good identification trait. Leaves, flowers and the shrub itself are all larger than those of mountain laurel. Unlike the cup-shaped mountain laurel flowers, rhododendron flowers look like big azalea blossoms with which most folks are familiar. In fact, azaleas share the same genus name, "*Rhododendron*".

IN GSMNP

Like mountain laurel, rosebay rhododendron is an acid-loving, thicket-forming member of the Heath (Ericaceae) family that often dominates the understory. Unlike mountain laurel, rhododendron prefers moist streamside forests and forests on protected slopes. It can be very abundant in the river cove forest, classic cove forest, acid cove-hemlock forest and cool cove forest. It can also be fairly abundant in the mixed oak-hickory-red maple forest of protected slopes, but it gives place to mountain laurel on the driest, poorest exposed slopes and ridgetops.

In the high elevation zone (4500'-6500+'), rosebay rhododendron is still fairly common in the northern hardwood forest and the red spruce-northern hardwood forest. It extends in fewer numbers up into the spruce-fir forest and even into the Fraser fir forest, though it is likely to be found only on south-facing slopes. Here and on heath balds it may share growing space with its relatives, Catawba rhododendron and Carolina rhododendron.

Allegheny Serviceberry
(Amelanchier laevis)

DESCRIPTION

Shade Tolerance =Tolerant
Soil Moisture Niche =Moist-Dry
Vertical Preference =Understory

Two species of serviceberry grow in GSMNP. Downy serviceberry *(Amelanchier arborea),* a tree of the lowlands, is rare, occurring in only a few of the Park's forest types. Allegheny serviceberry, is much more common. A tree of the Appalachian Mountains, its range extends north into southern Canada and south through the Smokies.

Both serviceberries have alternate toothed leaves. The leaves are oval shaped and frequently have a heart-shaped (cordate) base. Serviceberry bark is dark gray to black with distinctive black vertical slits that help identify it.

Serviceberry can be confused with mountain holly. Unlike serviceberry, mountain holly leaves have sunken veins. That is, they look like they are sunken slightly below the leaf surface. The leaves of mountain holly don't have heart-shaped bases. Mountain holly bark does not exhibit the black vertical slits of serviceberry either.

Serviceberry produces white flowers very early in spring, a characteristic from which its name derives. In earlier times, circuit preachers carried the Gospel to the mountains, arriving each spring about the time serviceberry blooms to perform funeral and wedding services relating to events of the previous winter. When serviceberry bloomed, folks knew the preacher would soon follow.

Serviceberry fruit, a reddish to purple berry-shaped pome is edible and delicious.

IN GSMNP

A shade tolerant understory tree, serviceberry seldom exceeds 30 feet in height. It is most abundant in the high elevation zone where it inhabits all forest types except the Fraser fir forest. In the middle elevation zone, serviceberry is often found in the northern red oak-hickory-red maple forest and in the acid cove-hemlock forest.

Sourwood
(Oxydendrum arboreum)

DESCRIPTION
Shade Tolerance =Intermediate
Soil Moisture Niche =Dry, Acidic
Vertical Preference =Subcanopy

Sourwood leaves are long, narrow and finely toothed. They could be confused with those of black cherry, but cherries have smooth gray bark while sourwoods have reddish-brown deeply ridged bark. They could be confused with those of serviceberry, but serviceberry bark is fairly smooth with black vertical slits. They could be confused with American chestnut, but chestnut leaves have large jagged teeth, while sourwood teeth are very small.

The name sourwood comes from the tart taste of the leaf midrib, in stark contrast to the sweet honey produced by bees from the flowers.

The distinctive bark of mature sourwood trees breaks into pronounced reddish-brown ridges separated by deep furrows. Jane (she knows who she is) calls it topographic bark. The tree's growth form is also a good id key. Sourwood trunks rarely grow straight, preferring instead to project upwards at an angle supporting an irregularly shaped crown, probably related to the tree's search for sunlight. Look also for the beautiful sprays of small urn shaped white blossoms in summer. The sprays project downward appearing like the fingers of a gracefully posed hand. The flowers fall, littering the ground with white, but the sprays remain into the winter.

IN GSMNP
Sourwood is a member of the Heath or Ericaceae family along with rhododendrons, azaleas and mountain laurel. Like its relatives, sourwood tolerates acidic soils well. It also tolerates dry soils well. These characteristics have adapted sourwood for its main niche in the subcanopy of oak-hickory-red maple forests and oak-pine forests. It is much more common in low elevation forests than in middle elevation forests, and it is rarely found in high elevation forests.

APPENDIX 1. TREE TABLE
Shade Tolerance, Vertical Niche and Moisture Rating of Major GSMNP Trees

Shade Intolerant Pioneer Trees	Shade Intolerant Pioneer Trees	Shade Intolerant Pioneer Trees	Shade Intolerant Pioneer Trees	Shade Intolerant Pioneer Trees
Site Moisture	Dominant Canopy Trees	Dispersed Canopy Trees	Sub-canopy Trees	Under-story Trees & Shrubs
Dry Sites	Virginia Pine			
	Pitch Pine			
	Table-mountain Pine			
	White Pine	Sassafras		
	Black Locust	Black Cherry		
	Yellow Poplar	Pin Cherry		
		Cucumbertree		
		Black Walnut		
Moist Sites		Sweetgum	Boxelder	

234

Shade Intermediate Trees	Shade Intermediate Trees	Shade Intermediate Trees	Shade Intermediate Trees	Shade Intermediate Trees
Site Moisture	Dominant Canopy Trees	Dispersed Canopy Trees	Sub-canopy Trees	Under-story Trees & Shrubs
Dry Sites	White Pine			
	Black Oak			
	Scarlet Oak	Hackberry		
		Post Oak		
	Chestnut Oak	Blackgum	Sourwood	
	White Oak	American Elm		
	Northern Red Oak	American Chestnut		American Chestnut Sprouts
	Red Maple	Silver Maple		Allegheny Serviceberry
	Black Birch	White Ash		
	Yellow Birch	Green Ash		
	Sycamore (American sycamore)	Sycamore		
Moist Sites		River Birch		Hazel Alder

Shade Tolerant Trees	Shade Tolerant Trees	Shade Tolerant Trees	Shade Tolerant Trees	Shade Tolerant Trees
Site Moisture	Dominant Canopy Trees	Dispersed Canopy Trees	Sub-canopy Trees	Under-story Trees & Shrubs
Dry Sites	Red Spruce			
	Fraser Fir		Mountain Ash	Fraser Fir Seedlings
		Pignut Hickory		Azaleas
		Red Hickory		Mountain Laurel
		Mockernut Hickory		Mountain Holly
	Sugar Maple	American Holly	American Holly	Umbrella Magnolia
		Fraser Magnolia	Fraser Magnolia	Catawba Rhodo-dendron
		Mountain Silverbell		Rosebay Rhododendron
		White Basswood (Basswood)		Flowering Dogwood

Shade Tolerant Trees continued	Shade Tolerant Trees continued	Shade Tolerant Trees continued	Shade Tolerant Trees continued	Shade Tolerant Trees continued
Site Moisture	Dominant Canopy Trees	Dispersed Canopy Trees	Sub-canopy Trees	Under-story Trees & Shrubs
	Yellow Buckeye (Buckeye)	Bitternut Hickory		Alternate-leaf Dogwood
		Sugar berry		Witch Hazel
	Eastern Hemlock			Striped Maple
				Mountain Maple
				Hobble bush
Moist Sites	American Beech			American Hornbeam

APPENDIX 2. MASTER LIST OF PLANTS
Found In The Book
Trees sand Shrubs

Alpha. Name	Common Name	Abbrev. Used In Tables	Latin Name
Alder	Hazel Alder	----	*Alnus* serrulata
Ash	Green Ash	G. Ash	*Fraxinus pennsylvanica*
Ash	White Ash	W. Ash	*Fraxinus americana*
Basswood	White Basswood	Basswood	*Tilia americana*
Beech	American Beech	Beech	*Fagus grandifolia*
Birch	Black Birch	B. Birch	*Betula lenta*
Birch	River Birch	R. Birch	*Betula nigra*
Birch	Yellow Birch	Y. Birch	*Betula alleghaniensis*
Blackgum	Blackgum	Blackgum	*Nyssa sylvatica*
Black Locust	Black Locust	B. Locust	*Robinia pseudoacacia*
Blueberry	Several species	Blueberry	*Vaccinium spp.*
Blueberry	Highbush Blueberry	Highbush Blueberry	*Vaccinium corymbosum*
Boxelder	Boxelder	Boxelder	*Acer negundo*
Buckeye	Yellow Buckeye	Buckeye	*Aesculus octandra*
Buffalo-nut	Buffalo-nut	----	*Pyrularia pubera*
Cherry	Black Cherry	B. Cherry	*Prunus serotina*
Cherry	Pin Cherry	Pin Cherry	*Prunus pensylvanica*
Chestnut	American Chestnut	Chestnut	*Castanea dentata*

Cucumbertree	Cucumbertree	Cuc-tree	*Magnolia acuminata*
Doghobble	Highland Doghobble	Doghobble	*Leucothoe fontanesiana*
Dogwood	Flowering Dogwood	F. Dogwood	*Cornus florida*
Dogwood	Alternate-leaf Dogwood	A. Dogwood	*Cornus alternifolia*
Elm	American Elm	A. Elm	*Ulmus americana*
Fraser Fir	Fraser Fir	Fraser Fir	*Abies fraseri*
Hackberry	Hackberry	-----	*Celtis occidentalis*
Hickory	Bitternut Hickory	Bitt. Hick.	*Carya cordiformis*
Hickory	Red Hickory	R. Hick.	*Carya ovalis*
Hickory	Mockernut Hickory	M. Hick.	*Carya tomentosa*
Hickory	Pignut Hickory	Pig. Hick.	*Carya glabra*
Hobblebush	Witch Hobble	Hobblebush	*Viburnum lantanoides*
Holly	American Holly	A. Holly	*Ilex americana*
Holly	Mountain Holly	Mt. Holly	*Ilex monticola*
Hornbeam	American Hornbeam	Hornbeam	*Carpinus caroliniana*
Huckleberry	Bear Huckleberry	Huckleberry	*Gaylussacia ursina*
Magnolia	Fraser Magnolia	Fraser Mag.	*Magnolia fraseri*
Magnolia	Umbrella Magnolia	Umbrella Mag.	*Magnolia tripetela*
Maple	Red Maple	Red Maple	*Acer rubrum*

Maple	Mountain Maple	Mt. Maple	*Acer spicatum*
Maple	Silver Maple	Sl. Maple	*Acer saccharinum*
Maple	Striped Maple	Str. Maple	*Acer pensylvanicum*
Maple	Sugar Maple	Sug. Maple	*Acer saccharum*
Minnibush	Minnibush	Minnibush	*Menziesia pilosa*
Mountain Ash	American Mountain Ash	Mt. Ash	*Sorbus americana*
Mountain Laurel	Mountain Laurel	Mt. Laurel	*Kalmia latifolia*
Oak	Black Oak	Black. Oak	*Quercus velutina*
Oak	Chestnut Oak	Chest. Oak	*Quercus prinus*
Oak	Northern Red Oak	N. Red Oak	*Quercus rubra*
Oak	Post Oak	Post Oak	*Quercus stellata*
Oak	Scarlet Oak	Scar. Oak	*Quercus coccinea*
Oak	Shingle Oak	Sh. Oak	*Quercus imbricaria*
Oak	White Oak	W. Oak	*Quercus alba*
Pepperbush	Mountain Pepperbush	Pepperbush	*Clethra acuminata*
Pine	Pitch Pine	Pitch. Pine	*Pinus rigida*
Pine	Shortleaf Pine	Short. Pine	*Pinus echinata*
Pine	Table-mountain Pine	Tm. Pine	*Pinus pungens*
Pine	Virginia Pine	Va. Pine	*Pinus virginiana*
Pine	Eastern White Pine	W. Pine	*Pinus strobus*
Poplar	Yellow Poplar	Y. Poplar	*Liriodendron tulipifera*
Rhododendron	Carolina Rhododendron	Car. Rhodo.	*Rhododendron carolinianum*

Rhododendron	Catawba Rhododendron	Cat. Rhodo.	*Rhododendron catawbiensis*
Rhododendron	Piedmont Rhododendron	------	*Rhododendron minus*
Rhododendron	Rosebay Rhododendron	R. Rhodo.	*Rhododendron maximum*
Sassafras	Sassafras	Sassafras	*Sassafras albidum*
Serviceberry	Allegheny Serviceberry	Serviceberry	*Amelanchier laevis*
Serviceberry	Downy Serviceberry	----	*Amelanchier arborea*
Silverbell	Mountain Silverbell	Silverbell	*Halesia tatraptera var monticola*
Sourwood	Sourwood	Sourwood	*Oxydendrum arboreum*
Spicebush	Spicebush	Spicebush	*Lindera benzoin*
Spruce	Red Spruce	Red Spruce	*Picea rubens*
Sugarberry	Sugarberry	----	*Celtis laevigata*
Sweet-shrub	Sweet-shrub	Sweet-shrub	*Calycanthus floridus*
Sweetgum	Sweetgum	Sweetgum	*Liquidambar styraciflua*
Sycamore	American Sycamore	Sycamore	*Platanus occidentalis*
Walnut	Black Walnut	B. Walnut	*Juglans nigra*
Witch Hazel	Witch Hazel	Witch Hazel	*Hamamelis virginiana*

Non-woody Plants

Alpha. Name	Common Name	Abbrev. Used In Tables	Latin Name
Bee Balm	Crimson Bee Balm	------	*Monarda didyma*
Beechdrops	Beechdrops	------	*Epifagus virginiana*
Blackberry	Allegheny Blackberry	Thornless Blackberry	*Rubus alleghenien-sis*
Bloodroot	Bloodroot	-----	*Sanguinaria canadensis*
Blue Cohosh	Blue Cohosh	------	*Caulophyllum thalictroides*
Crested Dwarf Iris	Crested Dwarf Iris	------	*Iris cristata*
Dolls-eyes	Dolls-eyes	------	*Actaea pachypoda*
Dutchmans-breeches	Dutchmans breeches	------	*Dicentra cucullaria*
Galax	Galax	--------	*Galax aphylla*
Hepatica	Hepatica	------	*Hepatica acutiloba*
Indian Pipe	Indian Pipe	-------	*Monotropa uniflora*
Joe Pye Weed	Joe PyeWeed	------	*Eupatorium maculatum*
Lady's-slipper	Lady's-slipper	------	*Cypripedium spp.*
Partridge-berry	Partridge-berry	------	*Mitchella repens*
Spring Beauty	Sprint Beauty	------	*Claytonia virginica*
Squawroot	Squawroot	--------	*Conopholis americana*
Toothwort	Toothwort	------	*Dentaria diphylla*
Trillium	Trillium	------	*Trillium spp.*
Trout Lily	Trout Lily	------	*Erythronium americanum*

White Snakeroot	White Snakeroot	------	*Eupatorium rugosum*
Wild Ginger	Wild Ginger Little Brown Jug	------	*Asarum arifolium*
Wild Golden-glow	Wild Golden-glow	------	*Rudbeckia laciniata*
Woodfern	Intermediate Woodfern	------	*Dryopteris intermedia*

Alphabetical Index

6282353R0

Made in the USA
Charleston, SC
06 October 2010